Successful I.T. Projects

in

Word

P.M.Heathcote, B.Sc.(Hons), M.Sc.

Published by

Payne-Gallway Publishers

76-78 Christchurch Street

Ipswich IP4 2DE

Tel 01473 251097

Fax 01473 232758

E-mail payne_gallway@compuserve.com

Acknowledgements

I would like to thank Richard Woods for showing me many of the advanced features of Word in a complete reversal of the usual teacher-student relationship, and for going through all the exercises in the book. My husband Oliver has made an enormous contribution to the production of this book, which is really a joint effort.

Cover picture © "Touch" reproduced with kind permission from Lorna Wilson
Cover photography © Mike Kwasniak, 160 Sidegate Lane, Ipswich
Cover design by Edward Morgan

First edition 1998
A catalogue entry for this book is available from the British Library.

ISBN 0 9532490 4 2
Copyright © P.M.Heathcote 1998

Printed in Great Britain by
W M Print Ltd, Walsall, West Midlands

Preface

Why tackle a project in MS Word?

MS Word is in many ways an ideal software package for a student in their first term of an 'A' Level or Advanced GNVQ course in I.T. to use for implementing a project. The emphasis in the NEAB syllabus for a Minor Project, for example, is on 'the full exploitation of particular generic application software and the advanced facilities available within them'. At the same time, the student must develop skills in producing a system which can help to solve a real user's problems. The variety and scope of problems that can be solved using Word is not so great as to be beyond students embarking on an I.T. course, and yet the software offers sufficient facilities to satisfy the project requirements.

Is Word suitable for either a Major or a Minor project?

Word is a good package for the NEAB's Minor Project (IT03), but it is not versatile enough to use as the sole package for a Major Project (IT06), normally completed in the second year. It could be used in conjunction with MS Access, for example to produce mail merged documents using a data source created as part of a database project.

Do we need yet another Word book?

Although many students are sufficiently competent in Word to use it for documentation purposes, very few have any significant experience of its advanced features. Unfortunately any book that covers the advanced features of Word is almost certain to be upwards of 400 pages and cost a small fortune. This book is different – it tells you what you need to know as succinctly as possible and it's affordable!

Yes, but can the exercises be done on a network?

Yes! Creating templates and storing macros is always going to be a problem on a network with restricted write access, but this book is specifically designed for use on a typical school or college network with these restrictions. Nothing is ever saved in any directory except the student's own. This means that work should be easily transferable between a school and home computer, provided, of course, that the same version of Word is used on the two systems.

What version of Word does the book cover?

The book is primarily for Word 97 users. However, a whole section of the book is devoted to Word 6, and guidance is given to Word 7 users to help them complete all the exercises except, of course, those which make use of facilities not found in Word 7. This means that the book is quite suitable for users of Word 6, Word 7 and Word 97.

Why isn't a sample project included?

There's a good reason for that! Since there is not an absolute obligation in the NEAB syllabus to find a real user, some students might find it positively hindered their creativity to be given a sample project on a plate. Word does not lend itself, as for example Access does, to solving an infinite variety of problems, and once you've seen an "ideal solution" to a fairly standard problem it can be hard to move away from it. Enough guidance is given in Part 4 on putting together a project to enable all students to produce a first class project report without being too prescriptive.

So go to it!

Contents

Table of Contents

PART III

Part 1

Word Basics

Chapter 1 – Getting Started

Introduction

The purpose of this book is to teach you enough to produce a really good Information Technology Project using Word as the customised application package for the end user. You'll also presumably be using Word to document your efforts. In doing so, you'll probably learn to use Word far more effectively than you have before, as well as learning some advanced features that you never knew existed.

The problem with starting yet another guide to Word is that inevitably there will be some people who have never used Word and want help with the most basic functions like how to change the font size (*"Font? What's that?"*) and others who have been using Word since they were in Mrs Scott's Infant Class and know that this is going to be a total waste of time. Well, you'd have to be the world's number one nerd to know everything useful about Word, so please try and remain open-minded.

What level are you at?

It might be useful to try and find out who knows what in the class. Then, if you're already dropping off the top end of the scale, perhaps you could make yourself useful by helping some of the beginners, at least for the first few sessions.

Tick the box that applies to you:

☐ I have never used Windows before, let alone Word.

☐ I have used Word to type essays and letters, but I have never used Styles, Automatic Table of Contents, Tables, Format Painter or customised bullets. (How *do* you get those big square tick boxes?)

☐ I can do all the above but I haven't created a template, used macros, set up a menu or customised the toolbar.

☐ I can already do all of the above as well as a lot of other things and I really don't think I need to come to class for the next 8 weeks.

All I can say is, I've used Word to write several text books and in spite of that, I've learned about six really useful new features this morning just by playing around, browsing through other people's textbooks on Word and using the Help menu. I also learned a lot about advanced Word features from Richard Woods, one of my first year A Level IT students, last Thursday. So if you really do already know a lot about Word, please stick around and share your skills, and learn how to put all that knowledge to good use in compiling a Grade A project that you can be proud of.

Loading Word

The way that you load Word will depend on which version of Word you are working with and whether you are working at home or on a school or college network. There may be a button in the Main Window or Applications Window that you can click on, or you can click on the **Word** icon in the Office Shortcut Bar at the top of the screen if that is visible. In Windows 95 you can click on **Start** in the bottom left hand corner and select **Programs, Microsoft Word**.

The Word screen

There are three basic areas on the Word screen: the bars at the top of the screen, the document window and the bar below the document window.

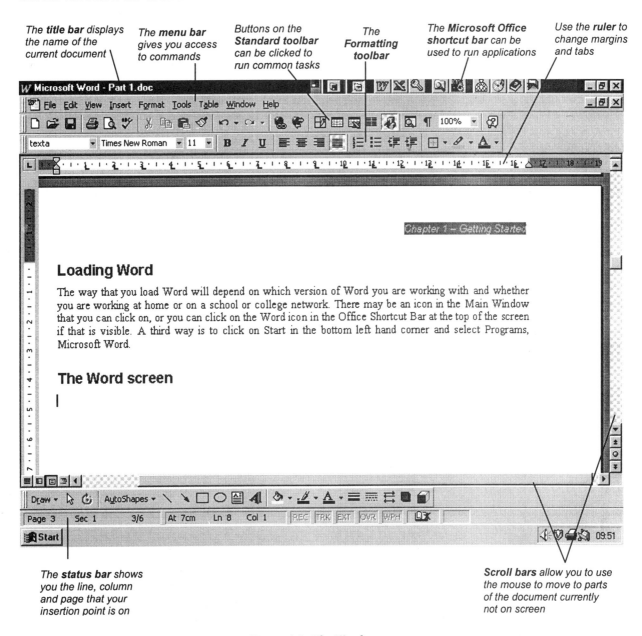

The **title bar** displays the name of the current document

The **menu bar** gives you access to commands

Buttons on the **Standard toolbar** can be clicked to run common tasks

The **Formatting toolbar**

The **Microsoft Office shortcut bar** can be used to run applications

Use the **ruler** to change margins and tabs

The **status bar** shows you the line, column and page that your insertion point is on

Scroll bars allow you to use the mouse to move to parts of the document currently not on screen

Figure 1.1: The Word screen

Task 1.1: Create, save and edit a document

In this exercise you'll open a new document, type some text and save it, and try out some of the buttons on the Standard toolbar. We'll also take a look at the **Edit** menu.

Opening a new document, entering text and saving it

- Click the **New** button on the Standard toolbar. The alternative way to open a new file is to select **File, New** from the menu bar.

- Type the first few lines of the text as shown in Figure 1.2, using the default font and point size, which is probably set to Times New Roman 10 point. I'm sure you don't need to be told not to press Enter at the end of every line. If you do, put your hand up and call for emergency help immediately.

Clinton deploys vowels to Bosnia
Cities of Sjlbvdnzv, Grzny to be first recipients

Before an emergency joint session of Congress yesterday, President Clinton announced US plans to deploy over 75,000 vowels to the war-torn region of Bosnia. The deployment, the largest of its kind in American history, will provide the region with the critically needed letters A, E, I, O and U, and it is hoped to render countless Bosnian names pronounceable.
"For six years, we have stood by while names like Ygrjvslhv, Tzlynhr and Glrm have been horribly butchered by millions around the world," Clinton said. "Today, the United States must finally stand up and say 'Enough'. It is time the people of Bosnia finally had some vowels in their incomprehensible names. The US is proud to lead the crusade in this noble endeavour."
Citizens of Grzny and Sjlbvdnzv eagerly await the arrival of the vowels. "My God, I do not think we can last another day," Trszg Grzdnjkln, 44 said. "I have 6 children and none of them has a name that is pronounceable by me or to anyone else. Mr Clinton, please send my poor, wretched family just one 'E'. Please."
Said Sjlbvdnzv resident Grg Hmphrs, 67: "With just a few key letters, I could be George Humphries. This is my dream."

Figure 1.2: Text entered in the default style

- Click the **Save** button on the toolbar. Alternatively, select **File, Save** from the menu bar, or use the shortcut key Ctrl-S. (This shortcut key is a really useful one to remember: use it every few minutes to save your work. Never work for more than 10 or 15 minutes without saving.) A window similar to the one shown in Figure 1.3 will appear:

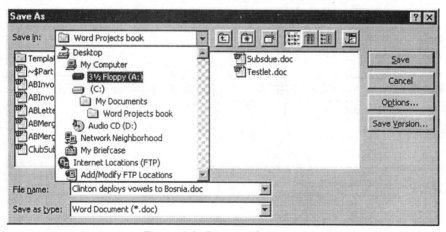

Figure 1.3: Saving a document

- Be sure to save to the *A:* drive or to your own personal area if you are working at school or college, by selecting the appropriate drive and directory from the Save In box at the top of the screen. (Use the Drives box and Directories box in Word 6.) Change the default name to *Bosnia.doc*.

  Notice that this dialogue box only appears the first time you save the document so that you can specify a name and drive location; the next time you press **Save**, it will automatically overwrite the older version. If you want to retain the older version unchanged, you should select **File, Save As** from the menu bar and then you can give the document a new name.

- Finish typing the text and save again.

Closing, opening and print previewing a document

- Select **File, Close** to close the document. If you haven't saved the latest changes, you will be asked if you want to save. Click **Yes**, and the document window closes. You can also close a document by clicking the Close Window icon **(X)** at the right hand end of the menu bar. Take care which Close icon you click, because the one in the top right corner will close Word as well, which you don't want to do.

- To open a document, click the **Open** button on the toolbar or select **File** from the menu bar. The latter is my preferred option because Word gives you a list of the last few documents you had open to select from and you just need to click the one you want. (See Figure 1.4.)

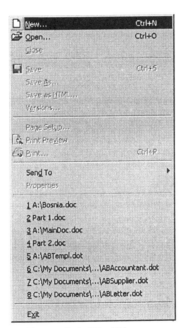

Figure 1.4: The File menu

- To see what the document will look like when printed, click the **Print Preview** button. This shows the current page at something between 29% and 35% of actual size. (Look along the Standard toolbar to the **Zoom** box, which displays 100% at full size and say, 35% in Print Preview.)

- Press the Escape key (marked *Esc* at the top left of the keyboard) to return to Normal view.

- You have probably identified the **Print** button by now, but in the interests of saving trees don't use this too often. It's preferable to use **File, Print** which gives you the option of printing only the specified pages, and setting various other options. There's no need to print yet.

Fonts and point size

How appealing your document looks and how easy it is to read will depend partly on the typeface, or font, you use. There are thousands of typefaces in existence but they can be grouped into two basic styles – serif and sans serif (meaning, literally, without serif). Serifs are the tiny appendages projecting from a letter. In this book, the paragraph headings are in a 14 point sans serif font called **Arial,** and the text is in an 11 point serif font, **Times New Roman**. Both these fonts are Truetype fonts, meaning that if the document is printed on a different printer from the one originally installed, the fonts will not alter and the page layout will remain the same. Truetype fonts have a symbol beside them to identify them and you are recommended to use only Truetype fonts in order to create portable documents.

Font size is commonly measured in *points*, with one point equal to $\frac{1}{72}$ of an inch. 8 points is about the smallest size that is easily legible, and you should definitely not use a point size of more than 12 for writing up your project.

Selecting text

Before we continue with the next few tools on the toolbar, just check that you know at least some of the smart ways to select text. These tips can save you hours of time.

Dragging the mouse

You can drag the mouse across all the text that you want to select. If the selection goes over several lines just drag straight down from the selection point and then across on the last line.

To select vertically, hold down Alt and drag down and across the text you want to select. This is useful for editing data in tabular form.

Selecting with the mouse

It's much quicker to click than drag. Try these shortcuts:

- Double-click a word to select it.
- Triple-click to select the paragraph.
- To select several paragraphs, place the cursor at the beginning of the text to be selected, press and hold down the Shift key, and click at the point where you want to end the selection.

Using the selection bar

The (invisible) selection bar is the left-hand margin of the document, next to the ruler. When you move the cursor into this area it changes to a right-pointing arrowhead.

- Click once to select the current line.
- Click twice to select the current paragraph.
- Click three times to select the whole document.
- To deselect the document, click in the right-hand margin.

Using the keyboard

- To select a single character next to the cursor use Shift and the right or left arrow key.
- To select a line at a time, press Shift and the down arrow key, or the up arrow key to select upwards.

- To select the entire document, press Ctrl-A (for All).

Spell-checking

Moving right along now, the next button is the spelling and grammar button – not used nearly often enough! You can either spell-check a selected portion of text or the entire document.

Make sure you have the English dictionary set as the default rather than the U.S. English dictionary, which will change all your spellings to the American version. To do this select **Tools, Language, Set Language**. In the Mark Selected Text box, click **English British** or **English (UK)**. Click **Default** and then **OK**. (You may not be able to change the default on a restricted access network.)

In Word 97 you can choose to have the grammar checker on or off – see Figure 1.5. (In Word 6, you can check grammar by selecting **Tools, Grammar** from the menu if this option is installed on your system.)

- Spell-check your document now.

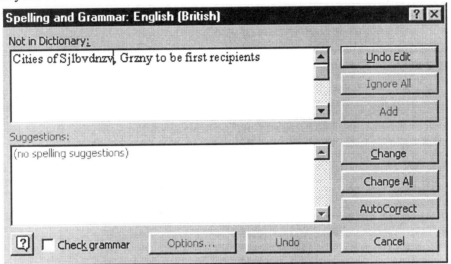

Figure 1.5: The spelling and grammar checker

Cutting, copying, pasting and undoing

The next three buttons are used for cutting, copying and pasting text. The corresponding keyboard shortcuts are Ctrl-X, Ctrl-C and Ctrl-V.

Try this exercise:

- Select the paragraph beginning *Citizens of Grzny* by double-clicking the mouse in the left-hand margin next to it.

- Click the **Cut** tool.

- Click an insertion point on a new line at the end of the document. (The *insertion point* is the point where the cursor is currently flashing on the screen, ready for text to be entered.)

- Press the **Paste** tool.

- Now undo this change by pressing the **Undo** tool twice (once for the **Paste** and once for the **Cut**).

You can undo and redo the last hundred actions. Cutting, copying, pasting and undoing can also be done by selecting from the **Edit** menu.

Using drag and drop for cutting, copying and pasting

This is a really useful shortcut.

- Select some text.

- Drag it to its new location.

- To copy text (i.e. insert a duplicate of the text instead of moving it), hold down the Ctrl key while you drag.

Other buttons on the toolbar

We'll look at the rest of the buttons (or at least the useful ones) in the course of the next few chapters.

Navigating around a document

Using the scroll bars is the most obvious way of scrolling through a long document. You can either click in the scroll bar or drag the box. The Word 95 Help system summarises the options, as shown in Figure 1.6. Word 6 is similar but does not have a Select Browse Object option.

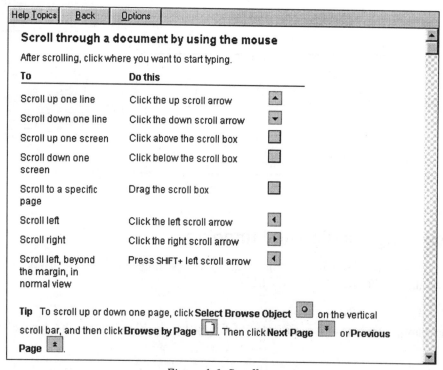

Figure 1.6: Scrolling

Keyboard shortcuts

You need a document of a few pages to try these out.

- Save your document before you change it in this exercise.

- Position your cursor at the beginning of each new paragraph and press Ctrl-Enter – this inserts a page break so your document is spread over several pages.

- Make sure that **View, Page Layout** is selected on the menu bar.

Now you can try out these shortcuts:

-	Ctrl-Home	Go to the beginning of a document
-	Ctrl-End	Go to the end of a document
-	Home	Go to the beginning of a line
-	End	Go to the end of a line
-	PgUp	Move up one screen of text at a time
-	PgDn	Move down one screen of text at a time.

The Edit menu

The **Edit** menu is shown in Figure 1.7. Options which are currently unavailable are greyed out – for example if you have just selected some text and copied it, **Paste** is available, but if nothing has been cut or copied to the clipboard it is greyed out.

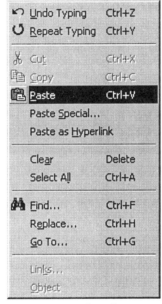

Figure 1.7: The Edit menu

You'll see that many of the functions that we have already looked at such as **Undo, Cut, Copy, Paste, Select All** can also be done by selecting options from this menu. We'll just look at **Find, Replace** and **Go To**. You can look in the **Help** system if you want to find out about the other options.

Finding and replacing text

Use this option to find all occurrences of a word or phrase in a document. For example, to replace *Clinton* by *Gore* throughout your text:

- Select **Edit, Replace**. The following dialogue box is displayed.

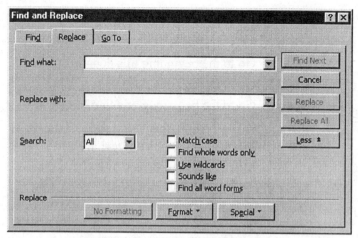

Figure 1.8: The Find and Replace window

- Type *Clinton* in the Find What box, and *Gore* in the Replace With box.

- You can either select **Replace All** to have all occurrences replaced without prompting, or **Replace** to be prompted before each replacement. Click **Replace**.

- The cursor moves to the first occurrence of *Clinton*. Click **Replace** to replace it. Do the same for each occurrence.

- Now you can practice undoing all your changes by pressing the **Undo** button until *Clinton* replaces *Gore* throughout.

You'll notice that there are various options like Match Case that you can select in the dialogue box, which are fairly self-explanatory, as well as further options like **Format** and **Special**. You don't really need to bother with these at the moment.

Note also that the Find What and Replace With boxes each save your latest entries in a drop-down list so you don't need to retype them if you need them again.

The Go To option

The **Edit, Go To** option provides another way of navigating round a document – really useful with a long document, when you can get to page 27 instantly without using the scroll bar. You can also use it to find a particular word or phrase in your document, like 'Chapter 27', 'Figure 18-1' or 'Rules of English'. Remember this for when you do your project documentation!

Return to the location of the insertion point

One final gem – this is a beauty! When you reopen a document you were previously working on and press Shift-F5, you will be returned to the location of the insertion point (i.e. the cursor position) when you saved the document. Or, if you are working on a document and have moved around, for example, press Shift-F5 to get back to where you were.

- Try this out, and then close the document without saving it – you don't want to leave it with the page breaks in it.

- Remember to bring your disk to the next session – you'll be working on the document again.

Chapter 2 – Styles and Formatting

The Formatting toolbar

In this chapter we'll look at some of the tools on the Formatting toolbar, and how to use them to smarten up the appearance of a document. You'll need to open the document *Bosnia.doc* that you created in the last chapter.

- Open *Bosnia.doc*.

- If you've forgotten your disk or didn't do this exercise, type the text now as shown in Figure 1.2.

- Make sure all the text is on the same page and in the default **Normal** style. If it is not, select all the text (triple-click in the left margin), click the arrow in the Style box to display the drop-down list of styles, and select **Normal**.

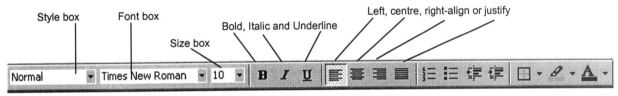

Figure 2.1: The Formatting toolbar

Using styles

The first box on this toolbar shows you the style that is currently being used. When you open a new document, by default Word uses a *template* (covered in detail in Part 2) named *Normal*, which contains several default styles.

Task 2.1: Format a document using styles and columns

- Select the top line by clicking in the left margin.

- Click the arrow in the **Style** box, and click **Heading 1** to apply the style.

- Select the second line and apply style **Heading 2**.

Creating your own styles

The default **Normal** style is Times New Roman, 10 point, left justified. We'll create a new style called **Story Text** which will be Arial 11 point, justified (i.e. straight edge down the right hand side of the page as well as the left side.)

There are several ways of creating a style. The simplest way is to change part of the text to the way you want it to look, and then give it a style name.

- Select the first paragraph by double-clicking in the left margin. Use the buttons on the Formatting toolbar to change it to **Arial, 11 point, justified**.

- It's a good idea to leave a little space between paragraphs. With the paragraph still highlighted, click the right mouse button to bring up the short-cut menu.

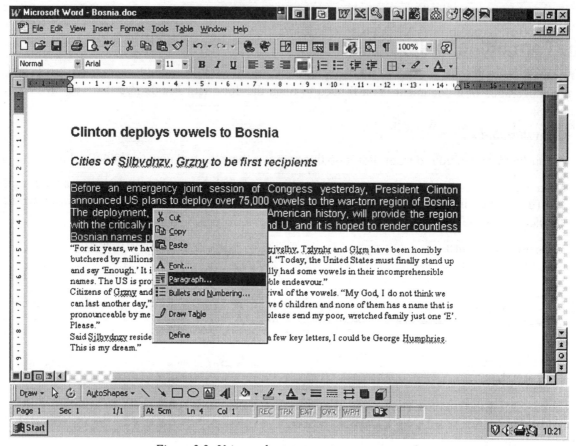

Figure 2.2: Using a short-cut menu to create a style

- Select **Paragraph** from the short-cut menu. This brings up another dialogue box as shown in Figure 2.3. (The dialogue box is slightly different in Word 6 and 7.)

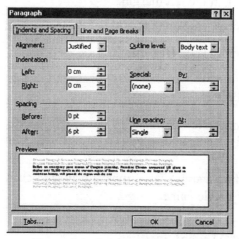

Figure 2.3: Paragraph formatting

Note that by clicking on the **Line and Page Breaks** tab (**Text Flow** in Word 6 and 7) in this window, you can turn hyphenation off, among other things. This means that words do not get automatically hyphenated at the end of a line, which some people dislike. On the other hand when using justified text, turning off hyphenation can lead to unsightly white space between words.

- Select **6 pt** in the Spacing After box and click **OK**.

- Click on **Normal** in the **Style** box and overtype it with the new name, *Story Text*. Press Enter.

- Select the rest of the story and change it to **Story Text** style by selecting this style from the style box.

Changing an existing style

You can change an existing style by selecting some text in the style, making changes, and then selecting the style name from the style box.

- Select the top heading.

- Change the font to **Times New Roman** and the size to **24 point**.

- Click the arrow in the style box, and select **Heading 1** from the drop-down list. In Word 97 the following dialogue box will be displayed. (In Word 6 and 7 the wording in the dialogue box is slightly different but the meaning is the same.)

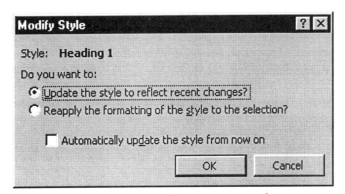

Figure 2.4: Updating an existing style

- Since you want to update (redefine) the style, leave the default selected and click **OK**. The **Heading 1** style is now permanently altered and any new text that you apply the style to will appear in Times New Roman 24 point.

- You can alter the formatting of a paragraph without permanently altering the style. Make the first paragraph bold.

Changing styles from the Format menu

Styles can also be changed from the **Format** menu, shown in Figure 2.5. Select **Style** from this menu, choose the style you want to modify, and follow through the various dialogue boxes.

Figure 2.5: The Format menu

Putting text into columns

You must be in Page Layout view to see text in columns. Select **View** from the menu bar and make sure **Page Layout** is selected.

- Select the remaining paragraphs starting with *For six years...* in the text.

- Click the **Columns** button on the Standard toolbar.

- Drag across two columns and click. The text is arranged in two columns.

- You can have a line between columns or adjust the width between the columns. Select **Format, Columns**. The following dialogue box is displayed.

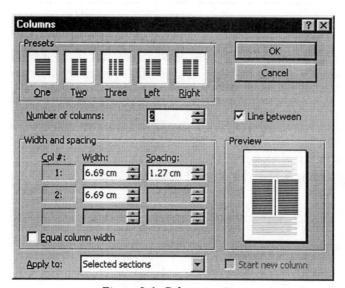

Figure 2.6: Column options

- Check the Line Between box. Your text should now appear as in Figure 2.7. If you can't see it all on the screen, try changing to 75% in the **Zoom Control** box on the Standard toolbar.

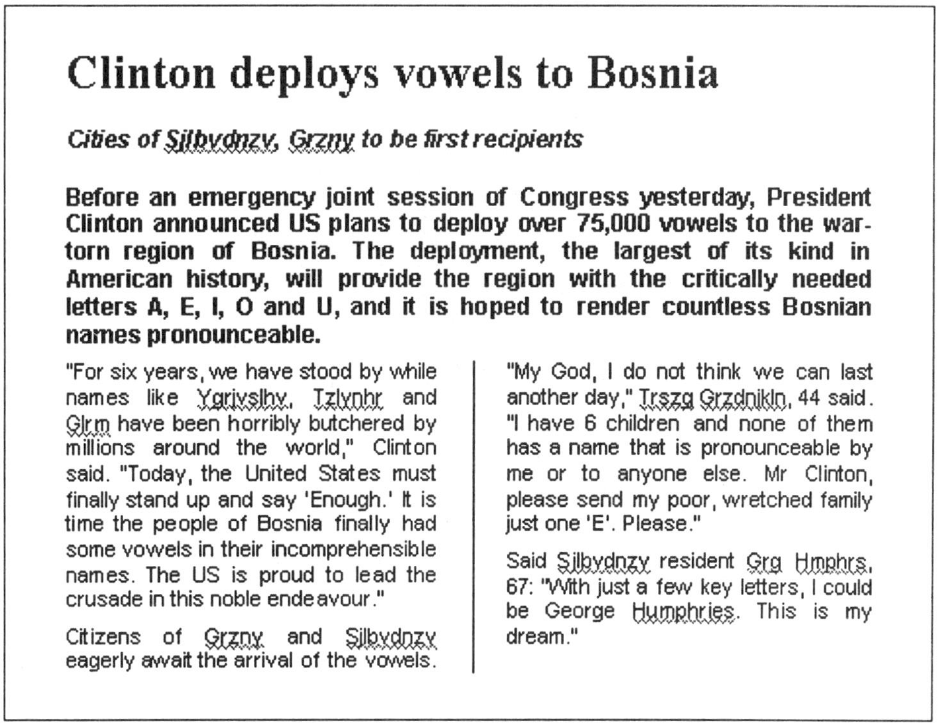

Clinton deploys vowels to Bosnia

Cities of Silbvdnzv, Grzny to be first recipients

Before an emergency joint session of Congress yesterday, President Clinton announced US plans to deploy over 75,000 vowels to the war-torn region of Bosnia. The deployment, the largest of its kind in American history, will provide the region with the critically needed letters A, E, I, O and U, and it is hoped to render countless Bosnian names pronounceable.

"For six years, we have stood by while names like Ygrivslhy, Tzlvnhr and Glrm have been horribly butchered by millions around the world," Clinton said. "Today, the United States must finally stand up and say 'Enough.' It is time the people of Bosnia finally had some vowels in their incomprehensible names. The US is proud to lead the crusade in this noble endeavour."

Citizens of Grzny and Silbvdnzv eagerly await the arrival of the vowels.

"My God, I do not think we can last another day," Trsza Grzdnikln, 44 said. "I have 6 children and none of them has a name that is pronounceable by me or to anyone else. Mr Clinton, please send my poor, wretched family just one 'E'. Please."

Said Silbvdnzv resident Grq Hmphrs, 67: "With just a few key letters, I could be George Humphries. This is my dream."

Figure 2.7: Text in columns

Drop caps

- To turn the first character of the story (the *B* of *Before*) into a drop cap, select it and then from the **Format** menu select **Drop Cap**. A dialogue box appears:

Figure 2.8: The Drop Caps dialogue box

- Select Dropped, two lines rather than 3 and press **OK**.

Small caps

- Select the word *For* at the start of the second paragraph of the story.

- Click the right mouse button to bring up the short-cut menu.

- Select **Font**, and check Small Caps in the next dialogue box. Click **OK**.

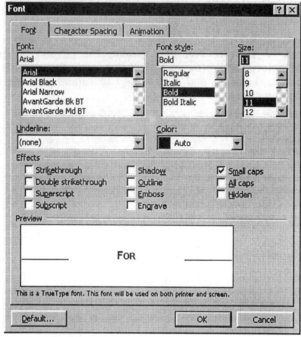

Figure 2.9: Setting small caps

The Format painter

The **Format painter** on the Standard toolbar is brilliant for applying an existing format to other parts of the document.

Often you have set the font, size etc of a particular heading and want several other headings in the same style without actually creating a style name. Or, you may want several isolated words in bold, italics or small caps, for example.

- Select the word **FOR** that you have changed to small caps.

- Click the **Format painter** once.

- Select or simply click in the first word of the next paragraph. It changes to small caps.

- To apply the same format to several different areas of text, first select text in the format you want to copy, then double-click the **Format painter**. Everything you select after that will have the format applied to it. Click the **Format painter** again to turn it off.

That completes this exercise. Save your work and close the document.

Chapter 3 – Tabs, Indents, Bullets and Boxes

Tabs

As soon as you open a new or existing document, you will see the ruler line with default tabs. There are four different types of tab stops: left, right, centred and decimal. It is easiest to set tabs from the ruler line.

Left hand tab stop
selected

Tab stops

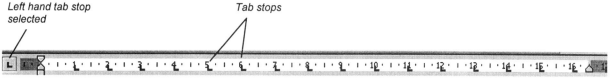

Figure 3.1: The ruler line

The tabs on the ruler line shown in Figure 3.1 are all left hand tabs one cm apart. If you were to set another tab stop, it would be another left tab, because the symbol for a left tab is showing at the left-hand end of the ruler line. (Measurements may be in either inches or centimetres – this can be changed using **Tools, Options,** clicking the **General** tab and making a selection in the Measurement Units box.)

Task 3.1: Create a price list using different tabs

Altering the default tabs

- Open a new document. The default tabs will appear faintly on the ruler line.

- Select **Format**, **Tabs**. The following dialogue box appears.

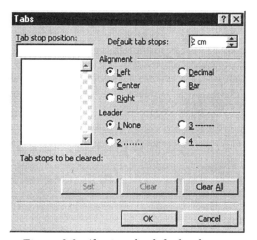

Figure 3.2: Altering the default tab stops

- Alter the default tab stops to **2cm**. Click **OK**.

- Type the following price list, leaving one tab stop between each entry, ignoring the fact that the entries don't line up correctly. Use Times Roman 11 point font. Save the document as *Prices.Doc*.

Optical Disk Cartridges

Manufacturer	Stock No.	Disk size	Bytes/sector	Capacity	Price (£)
Sony	ODC1556	3 ½"	512	128MB	8.40
Sony	ODC1557	3 ½"	512	640MB	30.95
TDK	ODC2334	5 ¼"	1024	1.2GB	34.95
3M	M567	3 ½"	512	230MB	8.95
3M	M569	5 ¼"	1024	2.6GB	53.75

Figure 3.3: Price list using default tabs

Note: In Word 7 and 97, if you leave a space after typing 3, before typing 1/2, it will automatically change to ½. In Word 6, you can make the 1 Superscript and the 2 Subscript to achieve the same effect. Alternatively, with Num Lock on, press Alt-0189 on the numeric keypad.

- Select the list. Then customise the tabs so that the list appears as shown in Figure 3.4. You can drag tab stops downwards off the ruler to get rid of them, and set new tabs by first selecting the type of tab you want in the box at the left hand end of the ruler line and then clicking on the ruler line. You can also drag a tab stop along the ruler line.

Manufacturer	Stock No.	Disk size	Bytes/sector	Capacity	Price (£)
Sony	ODC1556	3 ½"	512	128MB	8.40
Sony	ODC1557	3 ½"	512	640MB	30.95
TDK	ODC2334	5 ¼"	1024	1.2GB	34.95
3M	M567	3 ½"	512	230MB	8.95
3M	M569	5 ¼"	1024	2.6GB	53.75

Figure 3.4: Price list after some customisation

- Select just the heading line and alter the final tab stop so that the heading **Price** (£) is right justified. To do this, drag the last (decimal) tab stop off the ruler line, change the tab type to Right Tab in the box at the right-hand end of the ruler line and place a tab at about 11.5 on the ruler line.

Borders and shading

You can add borders and shading to your list.

- Select the whole list.

- Click the **Border** tool on the Formatting toolbar. We'll shade the heading as in Figure 3.6.

- Select the heading line of the table and select **Format, Borders and Shading**.
  Select the **Shading** tab, and the dialogue box shown in Figure 3.5 appears.

- Select a suitable shade and click **OK**.

Select this border

- With the top line only selected, put a border between the heading and the rest of the table. (In Word 6, clicking the **Borders** tool brings up the Borders toolbar and you can then select the appropriate border.)

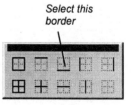

● Make the text bold so it stands out better.

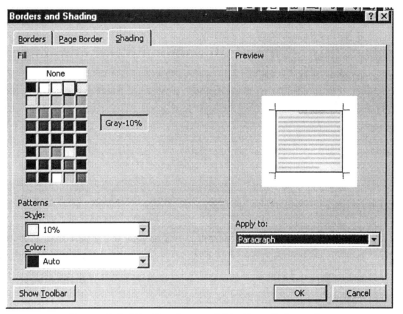

Figure 3.5: The Borders and Shading dialogue box

Changing indents

You can change both the left and right indent. In the figure below, the right indent marker has been dragged inwards to make the price list narrower. (The list has to be selected before doing this.)

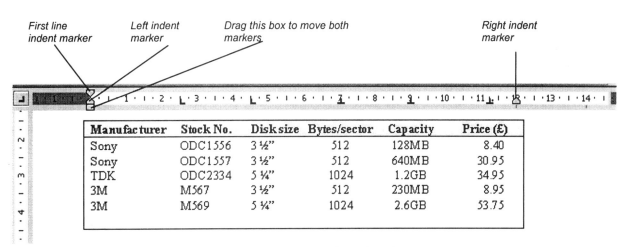

Figure 3.6: Altering the right indent

Note that Word gives you two different left indents. The 'First Line Indent Marker' is for the first line of a paragraph, and the 'Left Indent Marker' is for the rest of the paragraph. You can drag either marker separately or you can slide them together with the box underneath the indent marker.

Save your price list and close it when you've got it looking like Figure 3.6.

Hanging indents

Hanging indents are useful when you need to enter text in the format shown in Figure 3.7. With a hanging indent, the left indent marker (the one on the bottom) is to the right of the first-line indent marker.

Task 3.2: Create a tourist itinerary

This task brings together many of the topics already covered. Start by opening a new document and saving it immediately as *India.doc*. Remember to press Ctrl-S every few minutes while you are thinking what to do next.

---

14 NIGHTS / 15 DAYS ■ DELHI ■ ROHET ■ DEOGARH ■ UDAIPUR ■ DUNGARPUR ■ DHARIYAWAD ■ JUNIA ■ JAIPUR ■ DELHI

Rajasthan brings to life enduring images of a vibrant and proud past with fairy-tale forts and palaces gracing every horizon. A thriving folk culture expresses itself in an explosion of pageantry and colour, with exuberant festivals, dance and music. This tour combines the comfort of the country's finest heritage hotels with the comparative simplicity of the smaller forts of rural India, offering a superb insight into the depth and vitality of Indian culture.

Day 1 To Delhi: Fly from London to Delhi. Transfer to the Taj Palace Hotel for 1 night.

Day 2 To Rohet/Luni: Morning drive through Old and New Delhi, stopping at Presidential Palace designed by Edwin Lutyens, the Qutb Minar, the Red Fort and the Jama Masjid Mosque. In the late afternoon fly to Jodhpur and drive the short distance to Rohet/Luni.

Day 3 Rohet/Luni: This morning you will have an opportunity to take a jeep safari into the desert – a superb way to view the wildlife of the area such as blue bull antelopes, foxes and Indian Chinkara.

Figure 3.7: Travel Itinerary

Inserting symbols

- Start by typing the top paragraph using **Normal** text, ignoring the symbols and small caps for the moment, leaving two spaces between each place name.

  e.g. 14 nights / 15 days Delhi Rohet Deogarh etc

- You now need to insert the separator symbols. Place the cursor between *days* and *Delhi* and select **Insert, Symbol** from the menu. A window similar to that shown in Figure 3.8 is displayed.

- Check what fonts are available and select a suitable symbol to insert as a separator. (In Word 6, select the font **Dingbats** or **ZapfDingbats** to find a suitable symbol.) Click **Insert**. You can move the symbol window out of the way so that you can see what has been inserted.

- Move the insertion point to the next location that you want to insert a symbol, between *Delhi* and *Rohet*. You can just press Insert again in the Symbol window. Or, if you have closed the window, select **Edit, Repeat Symbol**.

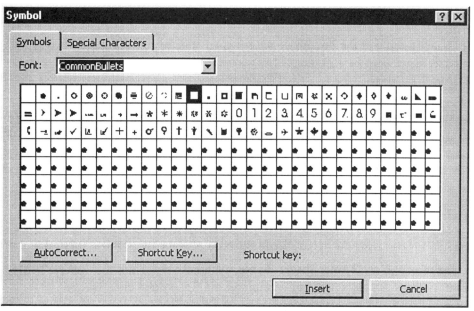

Figure 3.8: Inserting symbols

- Highlight the text, select **Format, Font** and make the text Bold, Small Caps. Press Enter twice at the end of the text before putting a box around it and shading it. (See Figure 3.7.)

- Type the next paragraph. (You'll need some text here because you'll be using this document again in Chapter 4.)

- Now you need to set the hanging indent. Notice also that the right hand is indented slightly in the Itinerary.

- Drag the indent markers as shown in Figure 3.9. Then enter the text. Don't bother making the first column bold yet, you're about to be reminded of a quick way to do that.

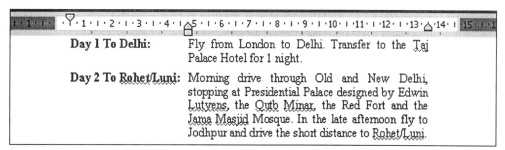

Figure 3.9: Setting indents

- To select just the first column, put the insertion point just before *Day 1*. Hold down the Alt key and drag across and down to highlight the first column. Then select **Bold** from the **Format** menu or click the **Bold** button on the Formatting toolbar.

- You can increase the left hand indent of any paragraph by first selecting it, or simply having the cursor somewhere inside the paragraph, and clicking the **Increase Indent** button on the Formatting toolbar. This increases the indent of the selected paragraph to the next tab stop. Clicking **Decrease Indent** does the opposite. (Put in a tab stop at the same point as the current left indent if you want to get back to where you started.)

Inserting a table

Next, you can insert a table at the bottom of your Travel Itinerary in *India.doc*. It will look like the one shown in Figure 3.10.

Prices in GB £'s per person sharing a twin bedded room				Departures on or between:		
Tour code	**Tour**	**Meal Plan**	**No. of Nights**	**1 Sep to 30 Sep**	**1 Oct to 18 Nov**	**19 Nov to 31 Dec**
RAJ20	Classic Rajasthan	RB	14	1250	1295	1375
RAJ21	Tour + Goa	RB/RO	19	2025	2075	2195
RAJ22	Tour + Shimla	RB/RO	18	1695	1725	1775

Figure 3.10: A table of prices

- Insert two blank lines underneath your travel itinerary and set the style to **Normal** to reset the indents.

- From the menu bar select **Table, Insert Table**. Alternatively, click the **Insert Table** tool on the Standard toolbar. Specify a table of 7 columns and 5 rows and click **OK**.

- Select the first four cells in the top row by dragging across them, and select **Table, Merge Cells**. Then merge the other 3 cells on the top row.

- Enter the text as shown, adjusting column widths where necessary by dragging the column dividers.
  Note: to add a new row at the end of the table, place the cursor in the last cell and press the Tab key.

That completes this task, so save and close the document.

Bullets and numbering

Task 3.3: Create bulleted / numbered lists

To create a bulleted list like the one shown below, click the **Bullets** tool on the Formatting toolbar. In this exercise, you'll be trying out different types of bullets and numbering.

- Open a new document and save it as *EngRules.doc*.

- Type the following text. (Click the **Bullets** tool after typing the heading and before typing the list.)

Rules of English

- Don't use no double negatives.
- Verbs has got to agree with their subjects.
- About them sentence fragments.
- Don't use commas, which aren't necessary.
- Try to not ever split infinitives.
- Using apostrophe's correctly is essential.
- Use the spell chequer to correct your speling.
- Make sure you haven't any words out.

Source: Unknown

Figure 3.11: A bulleted list

- To stop the bullets appearing, press backspace or deselect the **Bullets** tool before typing *Source:Unknown*.

- Now customise the bullets. Select your bulleted list, then select **Format, Bullets and Numbering**. A dialogue box something like the one shown in Figure 3.12 appears, though yours will probably have a different set of bullets.

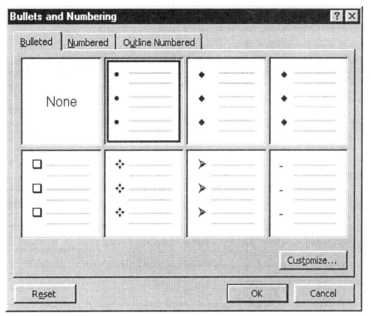

Figure 3.12: Selecting a bullet

- Click **Customise** (or in Word 6, **Modify**) to see a further selection. Another dialogue box appears:

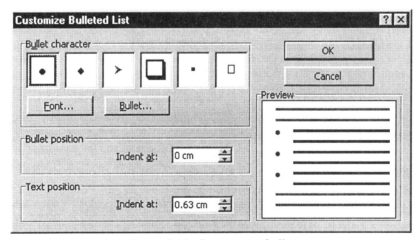

Figure 3.13: Customising bullets

- Note that as well as changing the size and shape of the bullets you can also specify the size of the indent. The default is probably fine, so just choose a bullet, click **OK** and have a look at the result.

- You can indent the whole list as before, using the **Indent** tool.

Numbered lists

Now you can turn your bulleted list into a numbered list. First select the whole text and copy it under the first list.

- Click the **Numbering** tool.

- Select the numbered list and select **Format, Bullets and Numbering**. Click on **Customise** (**Modify** in Word 6), and a new dialogue box appears as shown in Figure 3.14.

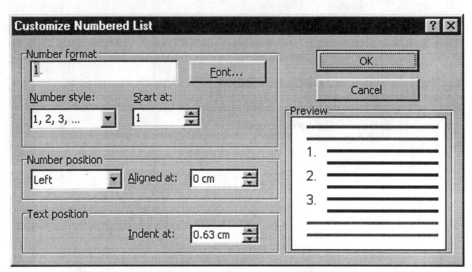

Figure 3.14: Customising a numbered list

- You can try out the various options. For example, try typing *Rule* in the Number Format box (in Word 6 and 7, the Text Before box) and selecting **1,2,3...** in the **Number Style** box.

Editing numbered lists

Numbered lists are useful because Word automatically adjusts the numbers for you when you shift things around.

- Select and drag Rule 7 up to point 1. The other rules will move down automatically.

- Insert a new Rule 4, by pressing Enter at the end of Rule 3 and then typing
  Just between you and I, case is important.

- Insert a new sentence fragment after Rule 5:
  And now for a few more...

- Turn off the numbering for this line. The numbers automatically adjust.

Note that if you wanted the numbers to start at 1 again instead of at 6, you can do this by selecting the line, selecting **Format, Bullets and Numbering**, and then selecting **Customize** to bring up the window shown in Figure 3.14. Then alter the number in the Start At box.

Checking Grammar

Now's a good opportunity to try out the grammar checker. Word 97 underlines spelling errors in red, grammar errors in green – although it doesn't find them all, and you may not agree with some of them. With the cursor in the word *Verbs*, press the right mouse button. Word gives you some suggestions, and you can click on one of them to have Word automatically change your text. If you don't agree with the suggestion, simply click **Ignore Sentence**.

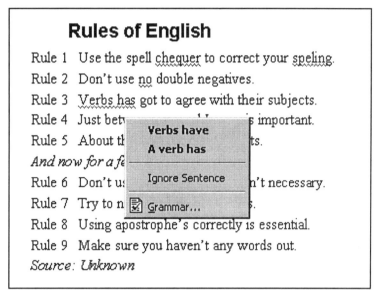

Figure 3.15: Grammar checking

In Word 6 and 7, select **Tools, Grammar** to check the grammar, but don't rely on it picking out all the errors!

That completes this task, so save and close the document *EngRules.doc*.

Chapter 4 – Graphics and Gridlines

Inserting artwork

You can use a picture from Word's clip art gallery to liven up a document, select an image from thousands available on CDs, or use a scanned photograph of your own. In this chapter we'll look at some of the techniques you will probably want to use in your project.

Task 4.1: Use graphics in a document

We'll start by inserting some clip art into the Travel Brochure created in Chapter 3 and saved as *India.doc*. Open the document and press Enter at the end of first paragraph of text (excluding the shaded box) to insert a new line. The clip art will be inserted at this insertion point. If you have not got the document handy, look at Figure 3.7 and type the first paragraph *Rajasthan brings to life …*

- Select **Insert, Picture, Clip Art** from the menu. A window similar to that shown in Figure 4.1 appears.

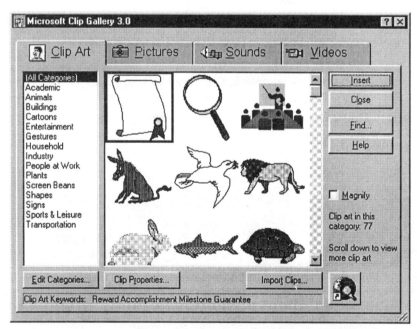

Figure 4.1: Inserting clip art

- Unfortunately there is nothing even remotely suitable to insert into the document, so pick anything – I've chosen a lion. (Are there lions in India?) The clip art picture is inserted into the document at the insertion point.

- You can size it by dragging one of the corner handles. If you drag one of the middle handles, the image will not retain its dimensions and will be distorted. Make the picture about a third of the width of the text.

- You can centre or right justify the picture by selecting it and using the tools on the Formatting toolbar. In Word 97 you can move the picture sideways by dragging inside it. (Stay away from the handles.)

Rajasthan brings to life enduring images of a vibrant and proud past with fairy-tale forts and palaces gracing every horizon. A thriving folk culture expresses itself in an explosion of pageantry and colour, with exuberant festivals, dance and music. This tour combines the comfort of the country's finest heritage hotels with the comparative simplicity of the smaller forts of rural India, offering a superb insight into the depth and vitality of Indian culture.

Day 1 To Delhi: Fly from London to Delhi. Transfer to the Taj Palace Hotel for 1 night.

Figure 4.2: Clip art inserted and sized

Positioning graphics

Try moving the picture vertically upwards. It jumps and inserts itself between other lines of the text. But suppose you want it, say, to the right of the paragraph.

- Select the picture and then click the right mouse button. (In Word 6 and 7, select **Frame Picture**. You will then be able to move the picture wherever you want it. To set Wrapping, right-click the graphic and select **Format Frame**. Set **Text Wrapping** to **None**. Then skip to Task 4.2.) In Word 97 select **Format Picture**, and the **Format Picture** window appears.

- Click the **Position** tab and the following window appears.

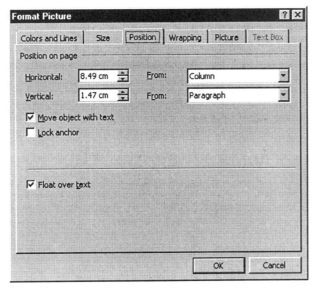

Figure 4.3: Formatting a picture

- Make sure the Float Over Text box is checked. Then click the **Wrapping** tab. You get a new window as shown in Figure 4.4.

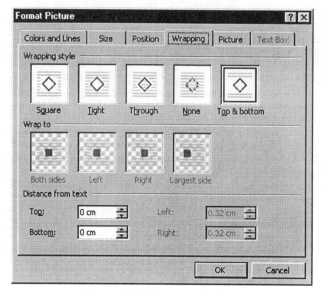

Figure 4.4: Wrapping options

- By default, Top & Bottom is selected, and the box shows you that the picture will be placed between lines of text. Click the Tight option, and the Wrap To options become available. Select Left, and click **OK**.

- Now you will find that you can move the picture to the right of the text.

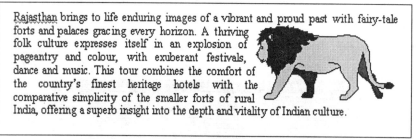

Figure 4.5: The graphic placed with a Wrap option

- Experiment with some of the other options!

Creating a watermark (Word 97 only)

While your graphic is selected, the Picture toolbar as shown in Figure 4.6 should automatically appear at the bottom of the screen. (If it doesn't appear, select **View, Toolbars, Picture**).

Figure 4.6: The Picture toolbar

A 'watermark' is a faint picture behind your text – or at least, it is in Microsoft's jargon. You can achieve this effect as follows:

- Insert another clip art image somewhere in the text, or copy your existing image to another location using Ctrl and drag.

- With the image selected, click the right mouse button, select **Format**, click the **Wrapping** tab and select None. Click **OK**.

- On the Picture toolbar click the **Image Control** button.

- Select **Watermark**.

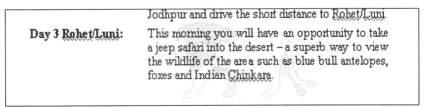

Figure 4.7: A watermark

Although it is possible to insert a watermark in Word 6 and 7, it's much more complicated and is not covered here.

That's the end of the first task! Save your document, but leave it on screen for the moment.

Task 4.2: Inserting, adjusting and labelling a screenshot

Taking screenshots

When you write up your project you'll need to write a user manual and this will probably need to include screenshots, pictures of buttons, labelled diagrams and so on. The best way to do this is to get hold of a screen capture utility program, often found as a freebie on the CD that comes with a computer magazine. However, you can capture a whole screen with Print Screen. This puts the screenshot on the clipboard, from where you can paste it into your user manual.

- With your *India.doc* visible on the screen, change to 75% view.

- Press Print Screen (near the F12 key).

- Open a new document.

- Type *User Manual* at the top of the page in style **Heading 1**, and press Enter a few times.

- With the insertion point under the heading, paste the contents of the clipboard. A full screen picture should appear.

You can now crop, size, and label this diagram as described below.

Cropping a graphic

In Word 97, select the graphic and use the **Crop** tool from the Picture toolbar to crop or shave the edges of the graphic. For example, to remove the bottom of the graphic, click the **Crop** tool and then click and drag the handle in the middle of the bottom border of the selected graphic.

In Word 6 and 7, the **Crop** tool is automatically activated when you press Shift and drag a handle.

User Manual

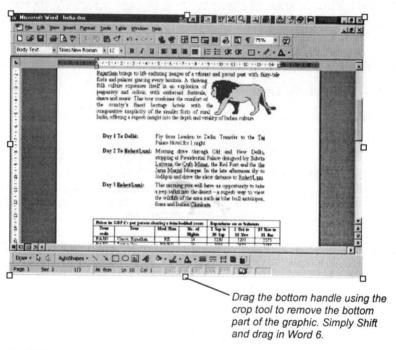

Drag the bottom handle using the crop tool to remove the bottom part of the graphic. Simply Shift and drag in Word 6.

User Manual

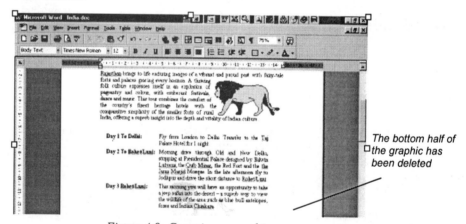

The bottom half of the graphic has been deleted

Figure 4.8: Cropping a graphic

The Drawing toolbar (Word 97)

(If you are using Word 6 or 7, please skip to the next paragraph headed *The Drawing Toolbar (Word 6)*.)

The Drawing toolbar is normally visible at the bottom of the screen. If it isn't, click the **Drawing Toolbar** button to display it. Alternatively, select **View, Toolbars** from the menu.

Figure 4.9: The Drawing toolbar(Word 97)

Select objects tool

Using the various tools on the Drawing toolbar, you can select a graphic, size it by dragging its handles, label it and so on. You can also draw various shapes and colour them from the palette of colours. You can experiment with all these tools – we'll just look at two ways to label parts of the graphic.

The label on the left hand side of the graphic in Figure 4.10 has been inserted using the **Autoshapes, Callouts** tool.

- From the Drawing toolbar, select **Autoshapes, Callouts** and select the second shape.

- Starting at the middle handle of the graphic, drag out a box.

- The arrow points the wrong way, so select **Draw, Rotate or Flip, Flip horizontal**.

- Adjust the position of the label.

- Use the **Fill Color** tool to fill the label with a white background.

- Insert the text in the box and alter the font, size and justification as required.

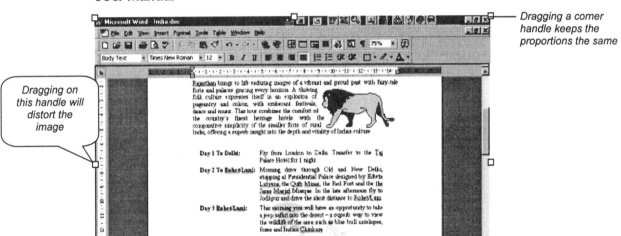

Figure 4.10: Labelling a graphic

The other way of inserting a label is to use the **Text Box** tool together with a line. This technique has been used for the label on the right in Figure 4.10.

- Select the **Text Box** tool and drag out a box where you want the label to appear.

- Insert the text and alter the font, size and justification as required.

- Select the **Line Color** tool and select **No line**.

- Select the **Line** tool and draw a line from the label to the corner handle. Lines look better if they are not just off the horizontal or vertical: you can ensure a horizontal line by holding the Shift key down while you draw the line.

This completes the task of inserting, adjusting and labelling a screenshot.

The Drawing toolbar (Word 6 and 7)

The Drawing toolbar in Word 6 is shown below.

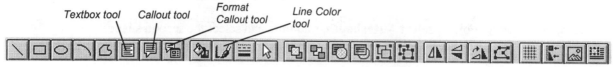

Textbox tool   Callout tool   Format Callout tool   Line Color tool

Figure 4.11: The Drawing toolbar in Word 6

- Use the **Callout** tool to create a label similar to that shown on the left of Figure 4.10. You can format the label using the **Format Callout** tool.

- Use the **Textbox** tool to create a tool similar to the one on the right hand side of Figure 4.10. Use the **Line Color** tool to remove the border, and the **Line** tool to add a line.

- Insert the text and alter the font, size and justification as required.

This completes the task of inserting, adjusting and labelling a screenshot.

Task 4.3: Create business cards

Blank perforated business stationery like that shown in Figure 4.12 is available from many outlets such as Staples. Alternatively, you can put ordinary A4 card through a laser printer and cut it carefully yourself.

In this task you'll lay out a sheet of business cards using the dimensions of the stationery shown, though of course you can vary these dimensions to suit your own needs.

Figure 4.12: Business card stationery

- Open a new document and select **File, Page Setup**.

- Measure the margins of your chosen stationery carefully, or use the dimensions shown in Figure 4.13. Remember you cannot print right up to the edge of the page.

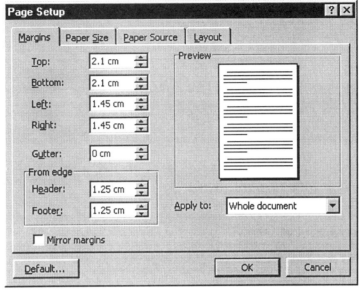

Figure 4.13: Setting margins for business cards

- Click the **Paper Size** tab and make sure that the paper size is set to *A4*. Click **OK**.

- Save the blank document as *BusCards.doc*.

- Measure the dimensions of the cards in your chosen stationery. In this exercise we will be getting 10 cards on the page, each 9cm by 5.1cm.

- Click **Draw** on the Drawing toolbar and select **Grid**. (If the Drawing toolbar is not displayed, select **View, Toolbars, Drawing**.) In Word 6 and 7, select the **Grid** tool.

- Set the grid to the dimensions of the business card as shown in Figure 4.14.

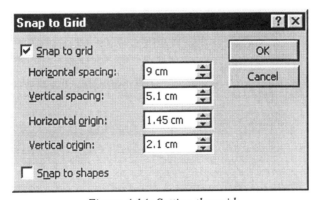

Figure 4.14: Setting the grid

- Make sure Snap to Grid is selected and click **OK**.

- Use the rectangle tool to draw a box in the left hand corner of the page. It will snap to exactly the right size. This box will just be used as a guide, and will be deleted later.

- Select **Draw, Grid** again and deselect Snap to Grid. Click **OK**.

- Use the **Text Box** tool (or Word Art in Word 97) to insert the Company name. Insert a name and address, telephone number etc and a clip art logo. You can probably improve on the design shown in Figure 4.15.

Figure 4.15: Design for a business card

- Select the border around the card and click the **Line Color** tool. Select No Line.

- With the **Select Objects** tool draw a box around the entire card so that the invisible border and all objects within the card are selected.

- Click the right mouse button and select **Grouping, Group**. This ensures that all the objects in the card will be treated as a single object.

- Now set the grid back to what it was originally (see Figure 4.14.) Make sure Snap to Grid is selected and click **OK**.

- Keeping the Ctrl key pressed and using the mouse, you can now copy the card 9 times to the rest of the page by dragging it. It will snap to the right place as soon as you are in the right area. You should end up with a sheet of 10 business cards.

- Save your document.

- Set the grid back to say 0.2 before you start working on another document.

Task 4.4: Save a document as Read-only

Saving a document as a Read-only file will prevent accidental alterations, and is a good idea for something like business cards which will almost never have to be altered – they will just be printed when required.

- If you have closed the *Buscards* document, open it again.

- Select **File, Save As** from the menu, but this time click the **Options** button. A new window appears as in Figure 4.16. (The window is slightly different in Word 6.)

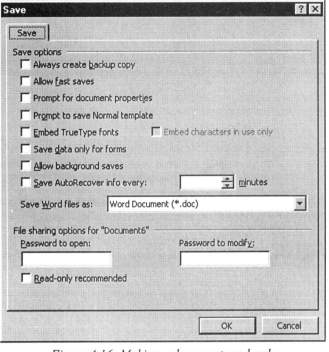

Figure 4.16: Making a document read-only

- Click the Read-only Recommended box.

- You can enter two different passwords, but you don't need to specify a password to open the document. Just specify a password to modify it – do choose something that is easy to remember, like 'modify'. This isn't a document vital to the security of the nation – you just want to prevent accidental changes. In Word 6, enter the password in the Write Reservation Password box.

- You'll be asked to confirm the password by reentering it. Type the password again, save the document as *Buscards.doc* and close it.

- Now select **File, Open**.

- You'll be asked for the password to open or modify it. If you only want to print it, just press the **Read Only** button. If you want to make modifications, type the password.

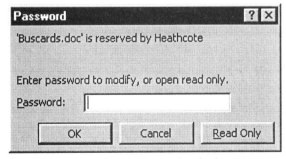

Figure 4.17: Opening a read-only document

Part 2

Advanced Skills in Word 97

In this section:

Chapter 5 – Headers and Footers

Introduction to Part 2

Part 2 is for those of you who will be using Word 97 to do your project work. If you are using Word 6, you can skip the whole of Part 2 and go on to Part 3. Part 3 contains exercises using the more advanced features of Word 6 which you will need to include in a Word project.

Word 7 falls somewhere between the two versions. If you are using Word 7, you should follow the instructions in Part 2 but sometimes you will be directed to the equivalent chapters in Part 3. (Check the logo in the right-hand margin.) This is the best way that I can think of to incorporate all three versions and I hope it won't cause too many problems for Word 7 users!

Working on a network with restricted access

Many students will be using a school or college network and will not have write access to files stored on the server. This poses various complications because Word generally expects you to save templates and macros in default locations to which you will not have write access. For example you may not be able to:

- Save customised templates in the default Templates directory;
- Create and save macros in the default *Normal.dot* template;
- Create and save customised menus and toolbars in the default *Normal.dot* template.

The first thing you must do, therefore, is to create your own template on which all other templates and documents will be based. This template will be called *ABNormal.dot* and will be saved in your private directory on the *A:* drive or wherever you normally save your work.

If you don't know what a template is or why you should need one, don't worry; templates are covered in the next chapter. Just follow along for now.

Creating your own template

> ### This is a very important step if you are working on a network!

- Select **File**, **New** to open a new file as a template, by clicking the **Template** radio button in the New dialogue box.

- Without entering any text, click **File**, **Save**. In the File Name box, type *A:\ABNormal.dot*. (Substitute a different pathname if you usually save your work in a particular directory.)

- Click **File**, **Close** to close the template.

Every document that you create in the exercises which follow will be based on this template. This way, you avoid any problems caused by trying to save in forbidden directories.

If you are working at home on a standalone machine and have full access rights, you can use default templates and directories but you will not be able to transfer your work to a school or college network. Therefore you are recommended to create the template above as suggested.

Opening a new document based on the new template

We now want to open a new document based on the new template. However, you will not be able to do this in the usual way unless your new template is stored in the Templates directory, and, of course, it isn't. We'll do it by attaching the template. (In Chapter 6 in Task 6.1 you'll learn another way of opening a new document based on a template that is not stored in the default Templates directory.)

- Select **File**, **New**. The only template available is 'Blank Document'. Click **OK**.

- We can now attach a different template to this document. On the **Tools** menu, click **Templates and Add-Ins**. (In Word 7, select **File, Templates**.)

- Click **Attach**.

- Select *3½ Floppy (A:)* or substitute the directory where you have stored the new template, in the Look In box. Enter *ABNormal* in the File Name box. Click **Open**.

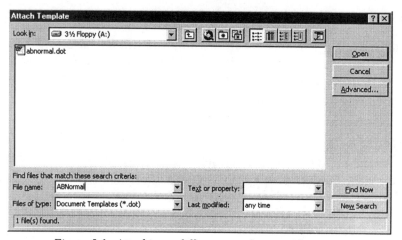

Figure 5.1: Attaching a different template to a document

- In the Templates and Add-Ins dialogue box, click **OK**.

- Save the document as *Maindoc*.

- Click **File**, **Save As** to save the document a second time as *ABMaster*.

Both these documents are based on the template *ABNormal*, and we will be able to save customised toolbars, menus, macros and anything else in our new template and they will be available in all documents based on the template.

Now that's done, the rest is easy!

Keep *ABMaster* open for the first exercise.

Headers and footers

A *header* is text or graphics that appears at the top of every page; a *footer* appears at the bottom of every page. A header is typically used to identify the section or chapter in a book, and the footer may contain the page number, a document identification of some kind, the author's name and so on.

Headers and footers are also useful when you are designing a letterhead for a club or company. The header can incorporate a logo and the organisation's name. The footer can include the company address (which could alternatively be placed in the header) and information such as the directors' names, VAT registration number and so on.

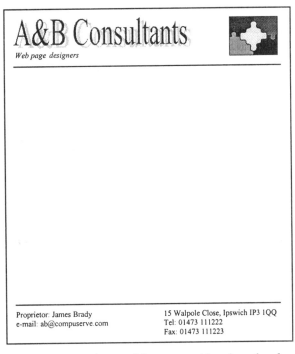

Figure 5.2: Headers and footers used in a letterhead

Task 5.1: Design letter stationery for a business

In this exercise you'll insert text, word-art and clipart into a header and footer to create a design for business stationery. You don't have to use the same Company name, address and logo – if you already have an end-user like a club or business in mind for your project, by all means use their details and use your own artistic talent to come up with a good design for stationery. As part of the project, you could create a few different designs and show them to the end-user who can then choose one.

It will make life easier if you save your documents and templates using the same file names as the ones used in this book though, as many exercises require you to open a particular document and do some more work on it.

Inserting a header or footer

- You should have the blank document *ABMaster.doc*, which is based on the template *ABNormal* (very important!) open on your screen.

- From the **View** menu choose **Header and Footer**. Word switches you into Page Layout view if you are not already there, and displays a screen similar to the one shown below:

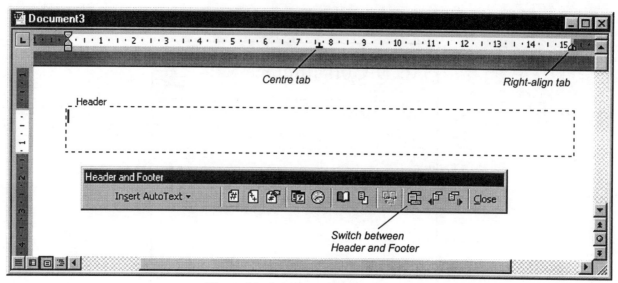

Figure 5.3: Inserting a header or footer

By default, you're placed in the Header area at the top of your current page. If you already have text in your document it will appear dimmed, in light-grey text.

The Header and Footer toolbar is displayed, with buttons to insert various items such as page number, date, time and so on. The only button you'll need for this chapter is the **Switch between Header and Footer** button.

Tip: You can also view and edit headers and footers by switching to Page Layout view and double-clicking the header or footer. The header or footer area will open.

By default, headers and footers are in Times New Roman, 10-point type. You can change this manually or by changing the header style as discussed in Chapter 2.

There are 2 default tab settings in the header and footer: a centre tab and a right-aligned tab. You can change these or add extra tabs as needed.

You can also use headers and footers to add a *watermark* graphic that appears on every page. (See Chapter 4.)

Use WordArt to insert a heading

MS Office comes with a supplementary application called WordArt which allows you to create interesting text effects to enhance newsletters, posters, letterheads and so on. (If WordArt is not installed on your computer, skip this bit and just type in a heading in 28 point Times Roman.)

To insert a special effect in your header:

- Position the cursor where you want the text (e.g. *A & B Consultants*) to be placed, and click the **WordArt** symbol in the Drawing Toolbar. (If this toolbar is not displayed, first select **View, Toolbars, Drawing**.)

- The WordArt Gallery window opens.

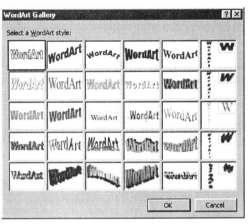

Figure 5.4: The WordArt Gallery

- Select your desired effect and press **OK**.

- A new window opens to allow you to type your text.

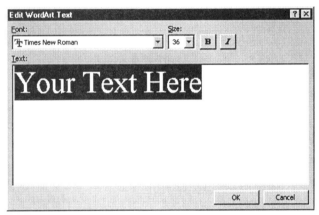

Figure 5.5: Entering WordArt text

- You can edit the text using the WordArt toolbar. (If the toolbar is not displayed, first select **View**, **Toolbars**, **WordArt**.)

- You can shrink or stretch the object by selecting it and dragging one of the corner handles, and move it by dragging (keeping away from the handles).

Inserting a text box

You can insert a text box using the text box tool from the Drawing toolbar. A cross-hair appears allowing you to make the text box the desired size, and you can then type text into it. Select the text and change the font size or typeface if you like. You can use the **Line Colour** tool to remove the border, and the **Fill Colour** tool to shade the box.

A text box can be used to insert a caption, such as *Web page designers* in Figure 5.2.

Inserting clip art

To insert clip art, either from the selection that comes with MS Office or from your own CD:

- Select **Insert, Picture, Clip Art** from the menu bar. A selection of clip art will be displayed.

Figure 5.6: Inserting clip art (Word 97)

- Select a suitable design and press **Insert**.

- Size the object as required and position it in your header. (In Word 7, use the **Frame** tool to frame the graphic so that you can move it, as explained in Chapter 4.)

- Use the **Line** tool to draw a line under the text. (Keep the Shift key down while you draw the line to ensure that it is horizontal.)

Working on the footer

Use the **Switch between Header and Footer** button in the Header and Footer toolbar to go to the footer. You can put the organisation's address, telephone number etc in the footer, or you may decide to keep the address in the header. It's up to you.

Press the **Close** button in the toolbar to return to the main document. Save your document *ABMaster.doc* and bring it with you to the next session as you'll be working on it some more.

Additional tasks

Make a decision on which organisation you are going to develop your project for. If business stationery is one of their requirements you will need to find out exactly what information needs to go on the letterhead. Work on designs for other stationery for your chosen organisation such as a 'With Compliments' slip, a Fax header sheet or business cards.

Chapter 6 –Templates

What is a template?

A **template** is a preformatted document to which you add text of your own. The headed stationery that a school or college uses, or a blank invoice form, are examples of templates.

When you create a new Word document, you are asked on which template you want to base your document. At that point, you are offered the default choice of *Blank Document* and you probably just click **OK**.

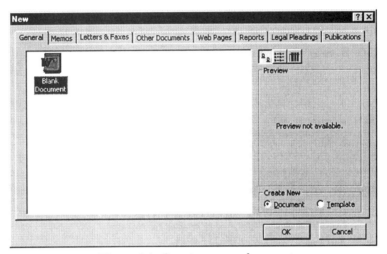

Figure 6.1: Opening a new document

However, Word also offers a range of other templates which contain preset information and styles for various different documents you might want to compose. For example, if you click on the **Letters and Faxes** tab, you are given the following options:

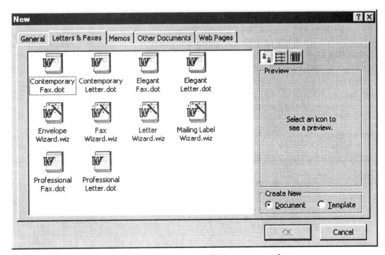

Figure 6.2: Letters and Faxes templates

Notice that you now have the choice of opening either a **Document** or a **Template**. If you want to use one of the templates to create your own letter, fax cover sheet or envelope, select **Document**. If you want to edit the actual template and save it under a different name as your own personalised template, choose **Template**.

Anything that you can put in a Word document can also be stored in a template. This includes:

- Text
- Graphics
- Macros
- Autotext (blocks of text that can be called up with a few keystrokes)
- Fields (e.g. current date)
- Font and paragraph formatting
- Styles
- Customised toolbars, menus and keyboard commands.

Creating a template

You can create a new template in several ways:

1. Select **File**, **New**, select an existing template, edit and save it. To edit an existing template, you must open it *as a template*, make the changes you want and then save it as a template (with a *.dot* extension) under the same or a different name.

2. Select **File**, **New**, select the *Normal* template, open a new document and add all the boilerplate text and graphics that you want to appear in the template. Then save it as a template. (*Boilerplate* text is simply text that appears in every document based on the template, like a letterhead.)

3. A variation on the second method is to open any existing document, delete anything that you do not want to appear in the template, and save it with a *.dot* extension.

We'll try all these three methods, and you can then decide which to use for your project.

Task 6.1: Use and edit an existing template

This task has two parts to it. Firstly, you will use an existing template to write a letter as follows:

- Open a new document using one of Word's existing templates.
- Try out the various features of the template.
- Type a short letter using the template.
- Save the letter as *Letter2.doc*, and close the document.

Secondly, you will edit the actual template, save it as a new template and then try it out, as follows:

- Open the Word template *as a template*.
- Customise it to your requirements.
- Save it as *AB Contemporary Letter.dot*.
- Open a new document using this template and type a short letter.

Using the *Contemporary Letter.dot* template

- Select **File, New** and click the **Letters and Faxes** tab. Choose *Contemporary Letter.dot* and click **OK** to open it as a document.

- The template will appear on the screen as shown in Figure 6.3.

- Click where indicated to type in a new company name, address and slogan.

- Type the recipient's name and address, e.g. *Mrs J. Fergusson*.

- Click on *Dear Sir or Madam* with the right mouse button. This brings up several alternative greetings, none of which are suitable. Delete the greeting and type *Dear Mrs Fergusson*.

- Type a short letter in place of the existing text.

- Type your name at the bottom of the letter.

- Save the letter as *Letter2.doc*

What you have just done is to use an existing template to create your own letter. However, you have not changed the actual template.

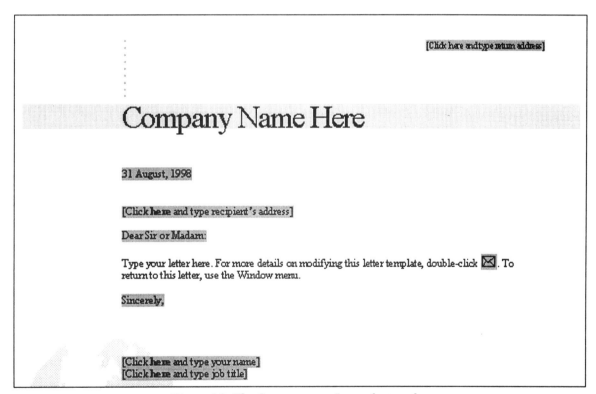

Figure 6.3: The Contemporary Letter.dot template

Editing an existing template

The next stage is to customise the template so that you do not have to retype your own company name, address etc every time you want to type a letter.

- Select **File, New** and click the **Letters and Faxes** tab. Choose *Contemporary Letter.dot* and this time, select **Template** before you click **OK**.

- The template will appear on the screen as shown in Figure 6.3.

- Click where indicated to type in a new company name, address and slogan. (The slogan goes at the bottom of the page in this template.)

- Edit the closing so that instead of *Sincerely* it reads *Yours sincerely* which sounds less American.

- Right-click on the word *sincerely* and a list of possible default 'closings' appears. Note that *Yours sincerely* is not one of them, and nor is *Yours faithfully*, commonly used in the U.K. when the letter starts *Dear Sir* or *Dear Madam*. We'll add these to the available alternatives.

  (In Word 7, you can edit autotext entries using **Edit, Autotext**.)

- Select **Create Autotext**. The following dialogue box appears:

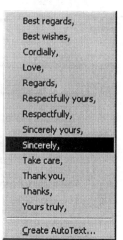

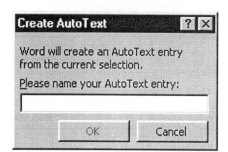

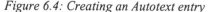

Figure 6.4: Creating an Autotext entry

- Enter the words *Yours sincerely* if they are not already displayed and click **OK**.

- Make another autotext entry for *Yours faithfully* as follows. First of all edit the words *Yours sincerely* to *Yours faithfully* in the letter. Then right-click and select **Create Autotext**.

Deleting autotext

Note that if you create autotext entries with spelling mistakes that you want to get rid of, you can do this as follows:

- On the **Insert** menu, point to **AutoText**, and then click **AutoText**. (In Word 7, use **Edit, Autotext** to edit the entry.)

- In the Enter AutoText Entries Here box, enter the name of the AutoText entry you want to delete.

- Click **Delete**.

Creating a new text style

The template contains several different text styles. Click on various parts of the letter such as the opening, body and closing. Although the styles have different names they are all Times New Roman 10pt. You may find this a bit small – you could change them all to 11 or even 12 point if you wanted to. We'll just change one preset style here.

- After *Dear Sir or Madam* at the head of the letter, press Enter. Notice that the style automatically changes to one called **Subject Line**, 9pt Arial. Click on **Format, Style**, to bring up a list of styles in the template. With the **Subject Line** style highlighted, select **Modify, Format, Font** and change the style to **Times New Roman 10 pt, Bold**. Click **OK** and in the Modify Style window select **Format, Paragraph** and make the Alignment **Centred**. Click **Apply** in the Style window to save the amended style.

Saving and using your template

- Save the amended template as *AB Contemporary Letter.dot*. If you are using a network with restricted rights, you will have to change the default destination drive and directory. If you are working at home, save the template in the default Templates directory.

If you are working at home, and have stored the template in the default location for templates, *C:\Program Files\MSOffice\Templates*, you will now be able to try out your template by selecting **File, New** from the menu and specifying your new template as the one to use.

However, if you are working on a school or college network, you will now have a problem! You are not given the option to use a template stored in any other directory. You can use the following method.

Using a template stored on the A: drive

- Minimise any documents and applications that you have running, including Word, to return to the desktop.

- From the desktop double-click on **My Computer**.

- Double-click on A: or wherever your template is stored.

- Right-click on *AB Contemporary Letter.dot* and select **New**. A new document based on the template will appear on your screen.

- Try using your template to type a short letter. Save it as *Letter3.doc*.

In the next chapter we'll write a macro to allow us to open a new document using a template stored in a directory other than the Templates directory. In the meantime, we'll look at the two other ways of creating a template.

Task 6.2: Create a template from an existing document

In this task you will create two templates:
1. A master template (*ABMaster.dot*) which will form the basis for all other templates such as a Fax header sheet and Invoice.
2. A letter template (*ABLetter.dot*) which will contain boilerplate text and styles suitable for writing a business letter.

The first part is very quick:

- Open the document *ABMaster.doc* which you created in Chapter 5. It should look similar to Figure 5.2, though you may have used a different company name, address, logo etc. (If you haven't created this document or have forgotten your disk, you need to go back to the beginning of Part 2 to create the *ABNormal.dot* template and *ABMaster.doc*.)

- Once you are happy with the header and footer, save the document as a template on the A: drive or wherever you normally save your files, calling it *ABMaster.dot*.

It's important to base all the templates around a single master template because later you will be storing macros and customised menus and toolbars in this template. Then they will be available to ALL templates and documents based on this one.

Now for the letter template:

- You need to have your template *ABMaster* open, which it will be unless you have just closed it.

- Select **File, Save As** to save the template as *ABLetter.dot* on A: or in your normal directory.

Inserting a date field

- Press Enter about four times, and then select **Insert, Date and Time**. Select a suitable format for the date.

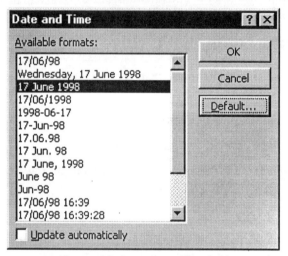

Figure 6.5: Inserting a date field

There is a problem with inserting the date using this method. If you check Update Automatically, then every time the document is opened, the date will be automatically updated to today's date. You want this to happen when you create the letter, but not when you load it up a week later to look at it. On the other hand, if you don't check Update Automatically, the date will always be displayed as the date you created this template.

The solution is to use a different type of field.

- Delete the date field you have just inserted.

- Click **Insert, Field**.

- In the Categories box, select **Date and Time**. In the Field Names box, select **CreateDate**. This will insert the date that a new document is created using this template, but it won't update it every time you reopen the document.

- Click **Options** and select *dd MMMM yyyy* or some other suitable format. This will display as, for example, 20 August 1998. Click **Add to Field** and then **OK**.

- The window should look like Figure 6.6. Click **OK**.

Figure 6.6: Using the CreateDate field

Adding a greeting, subject matter line, main body and closing

Delete any existing text in the letter.

- Under the date field, type the word *Dear*.

- Press Enter and create a new Subject Line style as follows:

- Select **Format**, **Style**, **New**. The following window appears:

Figure 6.7: Creating a new style

- The Style for Following Paragraph needs to be changed to **Normal**. You could alternatively create a different style for the main body of the letter, and then select that as the following style.

- Click **Format**, **Font**, **Bold**. Click **OK**.

- Select **Format**, **Paragraph** and select Alignment, **Centred** and Spacing **6pt** Before and After. Click **OK**.

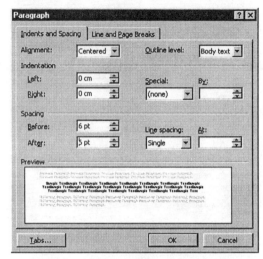

Figure 6.8: Setting the paragraph style

- Click Add to Template and then click **OK**. Click **Apply** in the Style window.

- Press Enter twice and then type the words *Yours sincerely*.

- Finally, place the cursor where the user would normally start typing – probably just above the date, where the recipient's name and address will be typed.

- Save your template *ABLetter.dot* and close the file.

Summary of templates hierarchy

At this stage you should have three templates stored in a directory to which you have full access rights:

ABNormal.dot - A blank template based on *Normal.dot*, the default Word template;

ABMaster.dot - A template based on *ABNormal.dot* containing the company header and footer;

ABLetter.dot - A template based on *ABMaster.dot*, containing boilerplate text for a business letter.

Any styles, custom toolbars, macros and shortcut keystrokes stored in *Normal.dot* will be available to all templates and documents based on *Normal.dot*.

Any styles, custom toolbars, macros and shortcut keystrokes stored in *ABNormal.dot* will be available to *ABMaster.dot* and *ABLetter.dot* and documents based on any of these three templates.

Any styles, custom toolbars, macros and shortcut keystrokes stored in *ABMaster.dot* will be available to *ABLetter.dot* and documents based on either of these.

Attaching a different template to an active document

In Part 1 you created Business cards using the *Normal.dot* template. If the *Buscards.doc* were to form part of your customised Word project, it would not display any custom toolbars or have access to macros and menus that you later create and save in *ABNormal.dot*. For it to do so, you need to attach the template *ABNormal.dot* to *Buscards.doc*.

When you attach a template, you can use styles, AutoText entries, macros, custom toolbars, and shortcut keystrokes from the template. Boilerplate text and graphics from the attached template are not available, however. To gain access to these items, you can copy and paste them from the template or create a new document based on the template.

- Open *Buscards.doc*. If you have previously made the file Read Only Recommended, type in the password *modify* or whatever you chose.

- On the **Tools** menu, click **Templates and Add-Ins**. (In Word 7, select **File, Templates**.)

- Click **Attach**, and then select *ABNormal.dot* from the A: drive or wherever you have saved it.

- Click **Open**.

Additional tasks

Create templates for your chosen organisation for their other stationery needs such as a Fax header sheet or Memo stationery mentioned in the last chapter. You should create them by opening the master template *ABMaster.dot*, making changes as needed and saving the new templates as, for example, *ABFax.dot*, *ABMemo.dot*.

Organise your work into different directories – one for your project work, one for exercises that you are doing separate from project work. Give careful thought to the naming of each file you save – a collection of files named *Letter1*, *Letter2* etc is an awful time waster, as a week later you will have to look through all of them to find the one you want. And while we're on the subject, LABEL YOUR FLOPPY DISKS with your own name, your course and a description of what the disk contains. You have absolutely no chance of ever seeing again an un-named disk that you accidentally left in the disk drive in your rush for the door at the end of last week's lesson.

Don't forget to take REGULAR BACKUPS.

Chapter 7 – Macros

What is a macro?

A macro is a series of recorded instructions that you can run using a single keystroke or by clicking a customised button on the toolbar, for example. You can record and save the instructions, edit them and assign them to a keystroke or a button to automate tasks that you frequently perform.

In this chapter you'll learn how to record and run a macro, view and edit the Visual Basic code that is automatically created, and attach the macro to a keystroke combination or customised button on the toolbar.

Word 7 users should do the exercises in Chapter 14 instead of the ones in this chapter (except 7.2).

Task 7.1: Create and edit a macro

Recording a macro

The first macro we will create will perform the following tasks:

1   Open a new document using the *Normal* template.
2   Display the heading '*Special Offer!!*' at the top of the page.

Before you record the macro you need to have a document open.

*   Open *Maindoc.doc*, which was created in Chapter 5. (It's essential that this document is based on the *ABNormal* template stored in your own directory if you are on a network – you won't be able to save macros in *Normal.dot*.)

To record the macro:

*   Select **Tools, Macro, Record New Macro**. Name the macro *OpenNormal* and type in a description as shown in Figure 7.1. (Note that macro names must begin with a letter and cannot contain spaces. Use a combination of upper and lower case letters to make your macro names comprehensible.) In the Store Macro In box, select *Documents based on ABNormal.dot*.

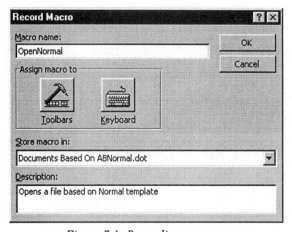

Figure 7.1: Recording a macro

Every keystroke you perform from now on will be recorded as part of the macro.

- Select **File**, **New**, *Blank Document* (on the **General** tab) and click **OK**.

- In large, bold, centred text, type ***Special Offer!!***, and press Enter.

- Stop the macro.

- Close the document you have just opened without saving it. You should be left with the original document containing the macro.

- Save this document (*Maindoc.doc*).

Running a macro

Now you can try out the macro.

- Select **Tools**, **Macro**, **Macros**. A window opens as shown in Figure 7.2.

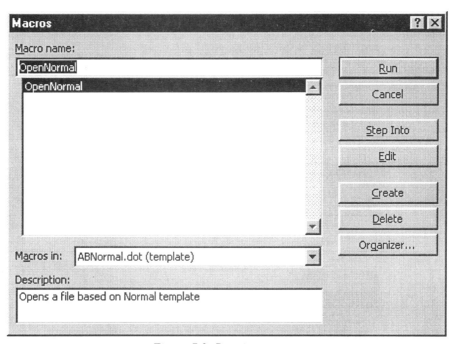

Figure 7.2: Running a macro

- In the Macros In box, select *ABNormal.dot*. In the Macro name box select *OpenNormal* and click on **Run**. A new document opens, and the text ***Special Offer*** appears.

You can close the new document without saving it.

Assigning a macro to a key combination

If you're going to use a particular macro often enough to be able to remember a keyboard shortcut for it, you can assign it to a key combination. You can either do this when you record the macro, by clicking on **Keyboard** in the Record Macro box (see Figure 7.1) or later as follows.

- Select **Tools**, **Customise** from the main menu bar. (Alternatively select **View**, **Toolbars**, **Customize** or right-click in the toolbar.) A window is displayed as shown below:

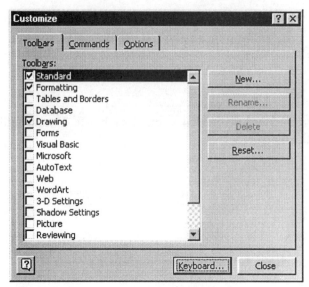

Figure 7.3: The Customise window

- Click on **Keyboard** at the bottom of the window. Another window appears. Select *ABNormal.dot* in the Save Changes In box, as shown in Figure 7.4. Scroll down in the Categories box, select **Macros**, and select the macro *OpenNormal*.

- With the cursor in the Press New Shortcut Key box, hold down the Alt key and press *SO* (for Special Offer). Click **Assign**. Click **Close**, and **Close** in the next window.

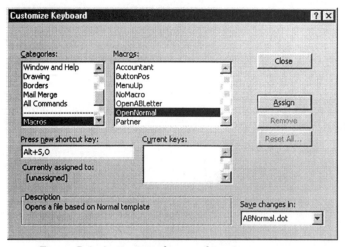

Figure 7.4: Assigning a key combination to a macro

- Try out your macro by pressing the shortcut key combination, *Alt-SO*.

Editing a macro

In the last chapter we created and saved a template. The problem was that unless the template was saved in the default Templates directory, it required special steps to open a new document that used this template. We're going to take the macro that we have just created and edit the code that was automatically produced to open a new document using the customised template *ABLetter.dot*.

- Select **Tools**, **Macro**, **Macros**.

- Select *OpenNormal* and click the **Edit** button. A new window appears as shown in Figure 7.5.

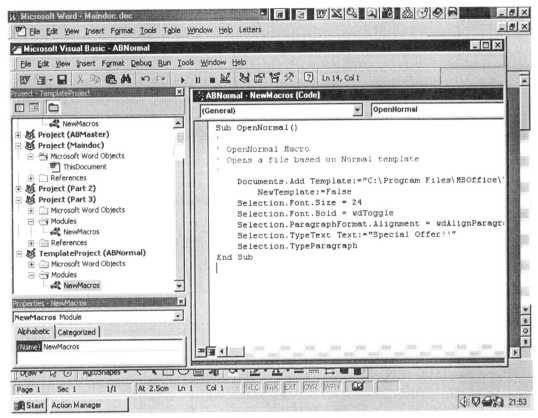

Figure 7.5: The Visual Basic window

The Visual Basic window is displayed. In the right hand part of the screen you can see the code that was automatically created when you recorded the macro. You can close the two other visible windows on the left and maximise the code window, so that you can see the code more easily:

```
Sub OpenNormal()
'
' OpenNormal Macro
' Opens a file based on normal template
'
    Documents.Add Template:= _
        " C:\Program Files\MSOffice\Templates\Normal.dot ", NewTemplate:= _
        False
    Selection.Font.Size = 24
    Selection.Font.Bold = wdToggle
    Selection.ParagraphFormat.Alignment = wdAlignParagraphCenter
    Selection.TypeText Text:="Special Offer!!"
End Sub
```

Note that a space followed by an underscore denotes the continuation of a statement onto the next line.

It is not hard to deduce that:

1   A macro begins and ends with the lines
```
Sub Macroname()

End Sub
```

2   Any line beginning with a single quote is a comment, and has no effect on the running of the macro. Comments are vital for documentation purposes and you should always include them.

3   The line
```
Documents.Add Template:="C:\Program Files\MSOffice\Templates\Normal.dot", _
     NewTemplate:=False
```

is the command which opens a new document using the *Normal* template. (The code is too long to fit on one line and continues on a second line.)

4   The remaining lines are the ones which cause the text to be typed and the Enter character recorded so that a new paragraph is started.

We want to create another macro that opens a new document using the template *ABLetter.dot*.

- Return to the document window by pressing Alt-F11. This acts as a toggle between the Visual Basic window and the document window.

- Select **Tools**, **Macro**, **Macros** and overwrite the macro name *OpenNormal* with *OpenABLetter*.

- Type a new description *Opens a new file based on ABLetter.dot.*

- Press **Create**.

- Copy the instruction which causes a new file to be opened and paste it to the new macro.

- Edit the line so that it reads
```
Documents.Add Template:="A:\ABLetter.dot", _
     NewTemplate:=False
```

The new macro should look like the one shown in Figure 7.6.

- Save the document.

- Return to the document by pressing Alt-F11.

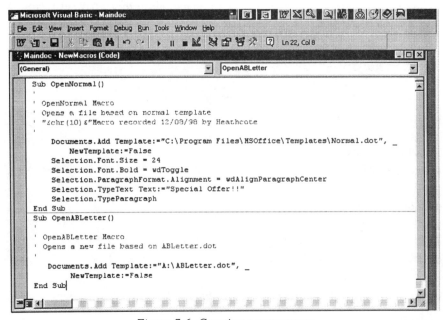

Figure 7.6: Creating a new macro

- Try out the new macro by selecting **Tools, Macro, Macros, OpenABLetter, Run**.

Task 7.2: Insert macrobutton fields into the ABLetter template

(Word 7 users can also do this!) We're going to effect a minor improvement in our customised template *ABLetter.dot*. You may remember that when you used the *Contemporary letter.dot* template in Chapter 6, there were several fields which you just had to click on and then insert text. This is achieved by means of a *MacroButton* field, which inserts a macro command that you can run by clicking the field. In fact the macro in this case doesn't need to do anything – the field is just there to be clicked on.

A *MacroButton* field is to be inserted which the user will click to type the recipient's name and address.

Creating an empty macro

- Open the template *ABLetter.dot* ready to be edited.

- Start by creating an empty macro as follows:
  - Select **Tools, Macro, Record New Macro**.
  - Name the macro *NoMacro*, since it will not have any actions attached to it.
  - Store the macro in *Documents based on ABLetter.dot*, and fill in an appropriate description: *Empty macro for use in letter template MacroButton field*. Click **OK**.
  - Stop recording the macro without performing any actions.

Inserting the MacroButton field

- Put the cursor a few lines below the header line, then select **Insert, Field, Document Automation**.

- In the Field Names box, click **MacroButton**.

- After the word MACROBUTTON in the box at the bottom of the window, type *NoMacro {Click HERE to insert recipient's name}* as shown in Figure 7.7.

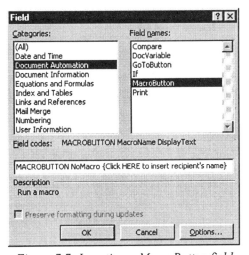

Figure 7.7: Inserting a MacroButton field

- Click **OK**, and the **MacroButton** appears as the text *{Click HERE to insert recipient's name}* on the letter. Don't click on it just now because you are creating the template.

- Now you can add another **MacroButton** field here with the message *{Click HERE to enter subject line}*. Follow the instructions already given for inserting a **MacroButton** field.

- Insert a third **MacroButton** field under the subject line with the message *{Click HERE to insert letter text}*.

- Save and close the template.

That completes the task.

Task 7.3: Attach a macro to a button on the toolbar

You'll like this bit! We're going to create a customised button which the user can click to open a new document using the *ABLetter* template. Make sure you have *Maindoc.doc* open before you start.

- Right-click on the Standard toolbar.

- Select **Customize** from the popup menu.

- Click the **Commands** tab in the Customize window, and select **Macros** in the left hand box. A list of macros appears on the right as shown in Figure 7.8.

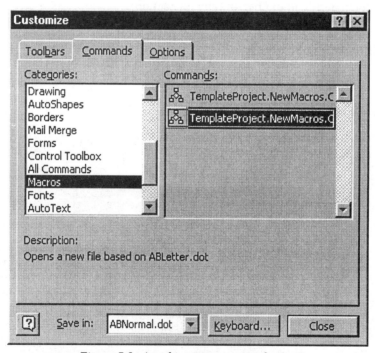

Figure 7.8: Attaching a macro to a button

- Make sure **ABNormal.dot** is specified in the Save In box.

- Drag the macro *Project.NewMacros.OpenABLetter* on to the end of the Standard toolbar. Drag it slightly to the right if you want a faint line to separate it from the button to its left.

- With the Customize window still open, right-click on the new toolbar item and type in a new name *Open Letter*. You can add a symbol to the button if you like using **Change Button Image**.

Figure 7.9: Customising a toolbar button

- Close the Customize window and try out your new button.

More detail on customising toolbars and menus is given in Chapter 10.

Task 7.4: Create a macro to print envelopes

When you've written a business letter, you obviously need an address on the envelope. There are basically three options:

1   Address the envelope by hand.

2   Use a window envelope and make sure the address is correctly positioned and the letter correctly folded.

3   Print the envelope.

The last option is a little tricky if you're using a network printer because the envelope has to be fed manually. However for a business user it is a useful thing to be able to do and Word makes it very easy.

Before creating the macro, try out the steps.

- Use your newly created button to open a new document using the customised template.

- Enter a name and address where indicated. You needn't bother writing the rest of the letter for the purposes of this exercise.

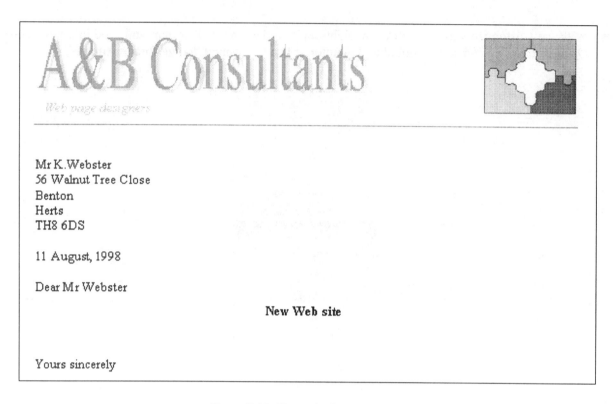

Figure 7.10: Using the letter template

- Select **Tools, Envelopes and Labels**.
- Select the Omit Return Address check box, as shown in Figure 7.11.

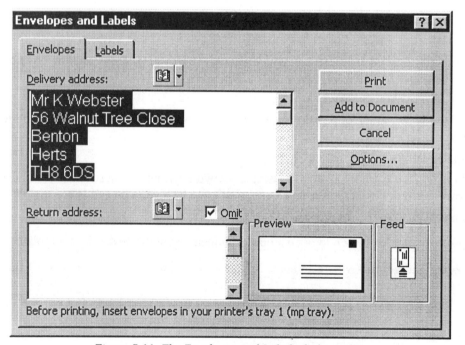

Figure 7.11: The Envelopes and Labels dialogue box

- You are instructed at the bottom of the window to put the envelopes into the correct tray. You may not be able to get this to work at school but it should be no problem at home, or for a user in an office.

- Once you have got all the steps to work, record them as a macro. Store the macro in *ABNormal.dot*.

- Attach the macro to a toolbar button marked **Envelope** in the current document. Select *ABLetter.dot* in the Save In box in the Customise window.

Note that you don't want this button to be available in all documents based on the template ABMaster – you want it to be available only when you are writing a letter.

- Save the document as *Letter with Envelope*. Save the changes to the template as well.

- Close the document, return to *Maindoc* and test your **Open Letter** button again. This time, the toolbar should display the **Envelope** button.

Using the Organiser to copy macros

Word uses the **Organiser** to copy styles, macros, toolbars and menus from one template or document to another.

- On the **Tools** menu, select **Macro**, **Macros**.

- Click **Organiser**. The following window is displayed:

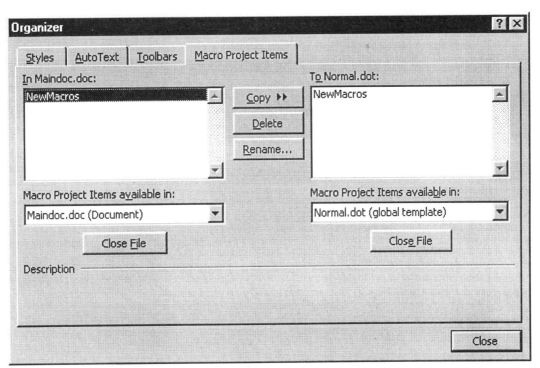

Figure 7.12: The Organiser

You can now copy a macro from one template or document to another.

Don't forget to use the Help system if you get stuck on some aspect of macros or anything else, for that matter!

Chapter 8 – Tables, Formulae and Forms

Introduction to invoicing

(Word 7 users should do the exercises in Chapter 15 instead of the ones in this chapter.)

Tables can be used in hundreds of different ways for all sorts of different applications. In this chapter we'll create an Invoice template which could be used to send out customised invoices for goods or services.

If you're going to do something similar for your project, you'll need to find out from the user what needs to go on the invoice. For example, if the annual turnover is greater than about £50,000 then the firm has to be registered for VAT and their VAT registration number needs to be displayed somewhere on the invoice. Find out the following:

- Is the firm VAT registered?
- Some goods such as books, are zero-rated, meaning that no VAT is payable. Will this firm be selling zero-rated or other goods, or a combination of both?
- Will the firm be charging for postage and packing?
- Are discounts given on any products?

You'll need to include the firm's name and address, the date, invoice number, the customer's order number, account number and address (and possibly a delivery address if this is different from the invoicing address), and details of the goods or services being invoiced. A possible layout is shown opposite.

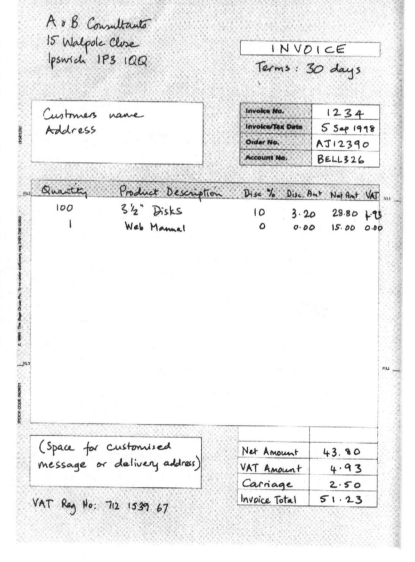

Figure 8.1: Invoice layout

There are hundreds of different ways of laying out an invoice so you need to consult your user, have a look at what is currently being used, and come up with a suitable design.

Task 8.1: Create a blank invoice form from a table

This task involves creating a blank invoice form to the design shown below in Figure 8.2.

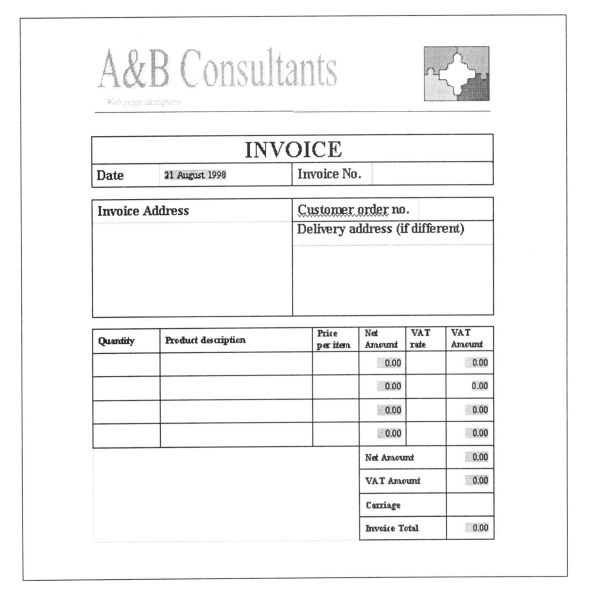

Figure 8.2: The Invoice layout to be created

Notes:

- *The footer containing the company address etc is not shown above but will be part of the invoice template;*
- *The user will delete the zeros in any unused rows of the invoice.*

Using the master template

It's a good idea for all the company's documents to have a consistent appearance, so we'll start with the master template and add boilerplate text to it to create a new invoice template.

- Load the template *ABMaster.dot* that was created in Chapter 6. This should contain just the company letterhead and footer.

- Save the template as *ABInvoice.dot*.

  (If you have not got this template handy, then for the purposes of this exercise, load a new document using the *Normal* template, put a company name and address in the Header, and save it without closing it, as *ABInvoice.dot*.)

Inserting a table and adjusting row height

There are two ways of inserting a table. One is to click the **Insert Table** icon and drag out the number of rows and columns that you want.

The second way is to choose **Table, Insert Table**. This is easier if you need more than about 6 rows.

- Select **Table, Insert Table** and specify a table of *6* columns and *12* rows, column width **Auto**.

  *Note that if you have inserted the table on the very top line of your document, and you later decide you would like to insert blank line above the table, you can do this by placing the cursor in the first cell and selecting **Table, Split Table**.*

- With the cursor somewhere in the table, choose **Select Table** from the **Table** menu.

- From the **Table** menu select **Cell Height and Width**. In the dialogue box set Height of Rows to Exactly **24 pt**.

  Note that you can also set the cell height in centimetres if you want to. Setting the cell to an exact measurement locks the cell size, which means that the cell will not expand if the user types more text than will fit in the cell, which could cause your form to spill over the page.

Merging cells and splitting the table

The invoice that we are creating from a single table contains cells of different sizes. Also, the main body of the invoice is separated from the top half containing headings and addresses etc.

- With the cursor in the top row click on **Table, Select Row**.

- Select **Table, Merge Cells** to turn the whole top row into just one cell.

- With the cursor in the top row select the **Centre text** button, **Times New Roman 24pt Bold** and type the word *INVOICE*.

- In the second row, type the word *Date* in the first cell. Set the style to **Times New Roman 14pt Bold**.

- Select the second and third cells and select **Table, Merge Cells**.

- Type the words *Invoice No.* in the next cell. Set the style to **Times New Roman 14pt Bold**.

- Merge the fifth and sixth cells in that row.

- With the cursor in the third row, select **Table, Split Table**.

You can widen the cell containing the words **Invoice no.** by dragging its right hand boundary. Similarly, you can adjust the width of the cell containing the word **Date**.

At this point, your invoice should look like Figure 8.3.

A&B Consultants

Web page designers

INVOICE			
Date:		**Invoice no:**	

Figure 8.3: The invoice taking shape

Styles and borders

We'll use the same style, Times New Roman, Bold 14pt for all the rest of the headings. Set a style called **Invoice Hdg** by highlighting the word **Date**, typing *Invoice Hdg* over **Normal** in the style box and pressing Enter.

You can customise the borders around cells or throughout the entire table. We need to remove the borders to the right of **Date** and **Invoice No.**

- Place the cursor in the cell containing **Date**, and select **Format, Borders and Shading**. The following window appears.

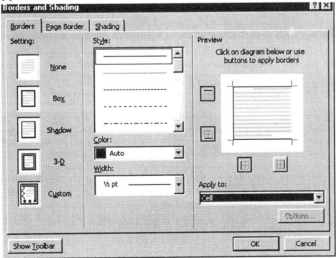

Figure 8.4: The Borders and Shading window

- Click on the right hand border in the diagram to remove it. Select **Cell** in the Apply To list box at the bottom of the window. Click **OK**.

- Place the cursor in the cell containing the words **Invoice No.** and select **Edit**, **Repeat Borders and Shading**.

Selecting cells, rows and columns

It is useful to be able to select individual cells in a table. You can then, for example, change the width of a single cell by dragging its borders, without affecting the rest of the column.

The Word Help system gives clear advice on this and many other topics. (Figure 8.5 was displayed using **Tables**, **Selecting Contents** from the Help Index.)

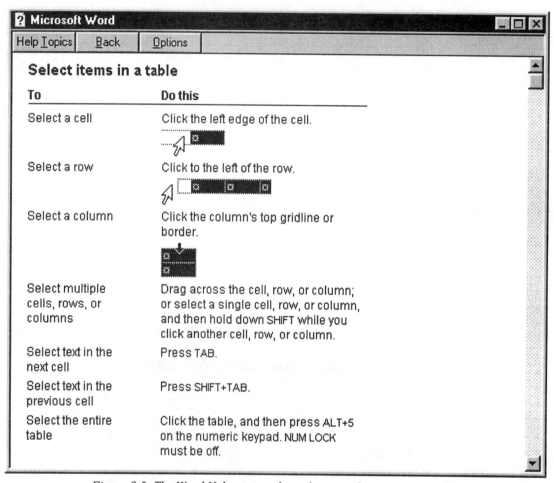

Figure 8.5: The Word Help system shows how to select areas in a table

Now that you know the basics of merging cells, splitting the table, changing column widths and borders, edit your table until it appears as shown in Figure 8.6.

A new style named **Invoice10** using 10pt Times New Roman has been defined for the column headings.

INVOICE					
Date			**Invoice No.**		

Invoice Address	**Customer order no.**
	Delivery address (if different)

Quantity	Product description	Price per item	Net Amount	VAT rate	VAT Amount

Figure 8.6: Changing widths of individual cells and columns

Inserting a default date

● With the cursor in the cell to the right of **Date**, select **Insert**, **Field**. In the Categories box select **Date and Time**, and in the Field Names box, select **CreateDate**. Click **Options** and choose a suitable date format. Click **Add to field** and then **OK**.

Inserting extra rows

We're going to need a few more rows, as the bottom part of the invoice will occupy 4 rows.

● With the cursor somewhere in the bottom part of the table, click the **Insert Row** button about 3 times to insert three new rows. Alternatively, you can select three rows of the table, and then select **Insert Rows** from the **Table** menu.

Changing the alignment of text in each cell

● Type the text *Net Amount, VAT Amount, Carriage* and *Invoice Total* as shown in Figure 8.7.

● Merge the other cells in the last 4 rows and remove the borders from the left hand corner cell.

● The text in the cells would look better if it was vertically centred in the cells. To do this, first select the 8 cells in the bottom right corner by dragging across them.

● Click the right mouse button and a menu appears as shown in Figure 8.7.

● Select **Alignment**, **Centre Vertically**.

- You can do the same for the rest of the table below the 'split' (i.e. starting with the row containing the headings **Quantity**, **Product Description**, etc).

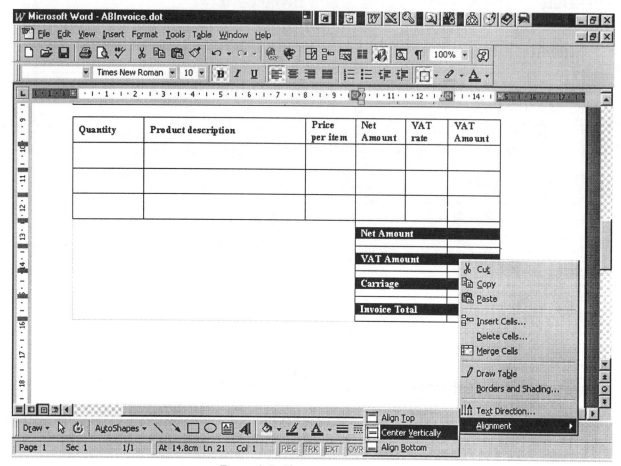

Figure 8.7: Changing text alignment

- Save your invoice template. We'll work on it some more in the next task.

Task 8.2: Enter formulae and test the invoice using test data

Test data

Look at the invoice now. The user will have to enter the information in the top part of the invoice, and also the **Quantity**, **Product description**, **Price per item** and **VAT rate** for each item. (Some items may attract VAT, others may be zero-rated.) We can enter formulae so that the Net and VAT amounts for each item are calculated automatically. The total **Net** and **VAT Amounts**, and the **Invoice Total**, will also be calculated automatically.

You need to make up some test data to test every part of the invoice. You need to calculate all the amounts manually so that you know whether or not you have entered the formulae correctly. This test data needs to be documented as part of your project.

Here is some sample test data for the invoice:

TEST DATA

Date: Today's date.   Invoice Number: 35

Invoice address: Mrs G. Bentham   Customer order no. 654321

                     5 Frederick Street   Delivery address:

                     Luton   8 Frederick Street

                     LU7 5RT   Luton

100 disks @ .32 each (17.5% VAT)

2 Manuals @ 27.50 each (0% VAT)

Carriage £2.50

Expected results: Net amount 32.00 + 55.00 = 87.00

                       VAT 5.60 on disks

                       Invoice total 95.10

Figure 8.8: Test data

The next stage is to enter the test data into the table.

- Enter the test data given above. Part of the invoice is shown in Figure 8.9.

Quantity	Product description	Price per item	Net Amount	VAT rate	VAT Amount
100	3 ½" disks	.32		17.5	
2	Web Manuals	27.50		0	

Figure 8.9: Test data entered into table

- You can immediately see that all these cells need to be formatted so that the data is centred vertically, so do this now, whether or not the cells contain data.

- Format all cells containing numbers so that they are right-justified, whether or not they currently contain any values. (Use the **Align-right** tool in the toolbar.)

We'll be entering formulae to calculate **Gross Amount** and **VAT Amount**, so leave the other cells blank.

Autocorrecting text

- If your first item appears as **31/2"** disks instead of **3½"** disks, it's probably because you didn't leave a space between 3 and 1/2.

- Check that the relevant Autocorrect option is turned on by selecting **Autocorrect** from the **Tools** menu.

- Click the **Autoformat** tab in the window and you will see the screen shown in Figure 8.10:

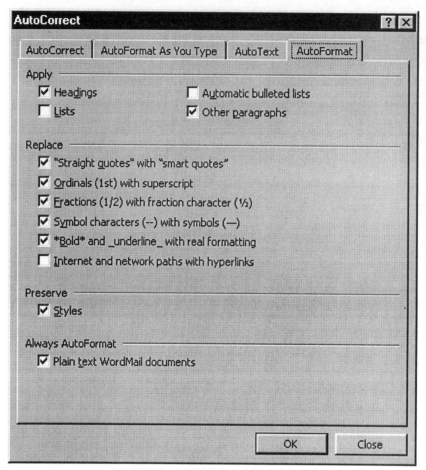

Figure 8.10: Autocorrect text

Entering formulae

Formulae can be entered into a table in Word in much the same way as in a spreadsheet, although rather more clumsily. The cells are referenced as in a spreadsheet, as A1, A2, B1 etc., starting in the top left corner.

Figure 8.11 shows some of the cell references. In cell D2, for example, we want to enter the formula

$$= A2 * C2$$

and in cell F2, the formula

$$= (D2 * E2) / 100$$

Qu A1	Product description		Price per item	D1	VAT rate	VAT Amount
10 A2	3 ½" disks	B2	C2	D2	E2	F2
2 A3	Web Manuals	B3	C3	D3	E3	F3

Figure 8.11: Cell references

- With the cursor in cell D2, select **Formula** from the **Table** menu. Delete the default formula and enter *=A2*C2*.

- Specify the number format as shown in Figure 8.12 and click **OK**.

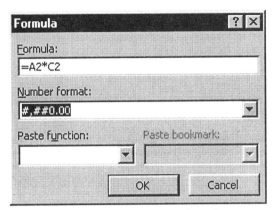

Figure 8.12: Entering a formula

- In cell F2 enter the formula *= (D2 * E2) / 100* and set the number format as above.

- Note that formulae in Word tables are always absolute, unlike in Excel, where you can enter relative references. You cannot therefore copy formulae to other cells and expect them automatically to adjust the cell references.

- Copy the contents of cell D2 to all the cells below it.

- You can toggle between the formula (field code) and the cell value by clicking in a cell with the right mouse button and selecting **Toggle Field Codes**. Do this now in cell D3.

- Alter the formula so that it references A3 and C3 instead of A2 and C2.

- Toggle back to the normal view.

*Note: You cannot insert field braces by typing characters on the keyboard. Fields are inserted when you use particular commands, such as the **Date** and **Time** command on the **Insert** menu, or when you press CtrlF9 and type the appropriate information between the field braces.*

Price per item	Gross Amount
.32	32.00
27.50	{ =A3*C 3 \# "#,##0. 00" }

Figure 8.13: Viewing the field code

- You may need to click the cell with the right mouse button and select **Update Field**.

- Copy the formulae in the top row to all other relevant cells and edit them all in the same way.

- In cell C8, for Net Amount enter the formula *=Sum (D2:D7)* or an equivalent formula depending on how many rows you have got in your table. Select the correct number format.

- In the cell below this, against **VAT Amount** enter *=Sum(F2:F7)* and select the correct number format.

- Enter test data of *2.50* for **Carriage**.

- In the bottom cell enter the formula =*Sum(C8:C10)* and select the correct number format. (Note that since some of the cells have been merged in this row, the cells you want to reference are in the C column rather than the F column.

The bottom part of the invoice should now look like Figure 8.14.

Quantity	Product description	Price per item	Gross Amount	VAT rate	VAT Amount	
100	3 ½" disks	.32	32.00	17.5	5.60	Cell F2
2	Web Manuals	27.50	55.00	0	0.00	
			0.00		0.00	
			0.00		0.00	
			0.00		0.00	
			0.00		0.00	Cell F7
			Net Amount		87.00	Cell C8
			VAT Amount		5.60	
			Carriage		2.50	Cell C10
			Invoice Total		95.10	

Figure 8.14: The invoice with formulae

Saving the invoice as a template

First of all, check that all the figures are correct (and your test plan will of course include some really thorough checking of every cell).

- Delete all the test data from the invoice (but not the formulae, which are shaded in grey).

- The fields do not automatically update. Right-click each one and select **Update Field Codes**. (Alternatively you can select the whole table first, then update the field codes.)

- Save the empty template as *ABInvoice.dot*.

Task 8.3: Add a customised button to update all fields automatically

Using the techniques learned in the previous chapter you can now add a button to the toolbar which the user can press to automatically update all the fields on the invoice.

- Press Alt-F11 to go to the Visual Basic screen.

- Make sure the Project Explorer and Code windows are shown on screen. If they are not, select them from the **View** menu.

- Double-click on **This Document**, under **Project(ABInvoice)**, **Microsoft Word Objects** in the Project Explorer window (see Figure 8.15).

- Select **Insert**, **Procedure** and name the procedure *UpdateFld*.

- Type the three lines of code shown in Figure 8.15, and save.

- Press Alt-F11 to return to the document window.

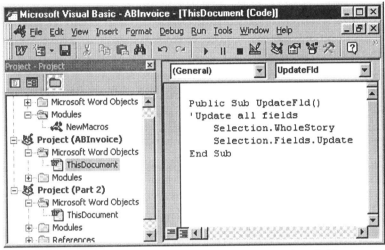

Figure 8.15: A procedure to automatically update fields

Adding a button to update fields

- Right-click in the toolbar, and select **Customize**.

- In the dialogue box, select the **Commands** tab, then **Macros**.

- Drag the macro name onto the toolbar, and right-click it to change its name to *Update Fields*.

- Close the Customize window, and save the template.

- Enter some test data and note that the fields do not automatically update.

- Press your new **Update Fields** button. Hey presto!

The manual processes involved

In your project work, you must consider HOW the user will use an invoice template such as the one you have created, and document this in the user manual. For example, the user may print out two copies of each invoice, one to send to the customer and one to keep in a file near at hand. When a new invoice is to be printed, the user can load the template, look up the last Invoice number used and enter the next number. The invoice can be saved as *Invoice147.doc* or whatever number it was, in a special Invoices directory. When the customer pays the invoice, the user can handwrite, for example, ***Paid 12/09/98*** on the invoice, and that way, keep track of who has not yet paid and send reminders for overdue invoices.

Such a system is really only suitable for a business sending out a small number of invoices – for more than about 3 invoices a week, I would recommend an Accounts system such as Sage Sterling for Windows!

Using Word to create a form

You have just created a template for an invoice, and have seen how to insert a formula into a cell. There are many other types of form that Word can help you to create, such as:

- An online order form;
- A multiple choice test or questionnaire;
- An application or enrolment form for a college course.

The first step in creating a form is to create a template containing all the basic information that is to go on the form, and any list boxes, check boxes, dialog boxes and Help features you want to include. The template may also contain Autotext entries and macros. You can then protect the areas of the form that you don't want a user to be able to change.

Task 8.4: Create a form to advertise special offers

In this task you will create a form which the user can fill in and print each week to advertise special offers on computers. The form when printed will look something like Figure 8.16.

This week's bargains

Model	Memory	Hard Disk	Speakers	Price	VAT	Total	Cash Discount
Tiny Pentium 266	8Mb	2GB	☒	£1,000.00	£175.00	1175.00	5%
Time 486	4Mb	1GB	☐	£600.00	£105.00	705.00	0%
Vector Pentium 166	16Mb	4Gb	☒	£999.00	£174.82	1173.82	0%
Time Pentium 300	32Mb	4Gb	☒	£1,350.00	£236.25	1586.25	5%

Figure 8.16: The printed form

Many forms are based around a table.

- Open the template *ABMaster.dot* and save it as *ABForm.dot*.

- Type the heading *This week's bargains* as in Figure 8.16.

- Insert a table of 8 columns and 5 rows.

- Type the headings as shown in Figure 8.16 and shade the top row. The row height has been set to **At Least 24pt** and all cells have been vertically centred. The headings in the top row are centred.

The Forms toolbar

Word has a special toolbar which enables you to insert different types of field anywhere on a form, set various properties and protect the form.

- Right-click the mouse on a toolbar and select **Forms** (or select **View, Toolbars, Forms**).

The Forms toolbar appears as shown in Figure 8.17.

Figure 8.17: The Forms toolbar

When you create a form template, you must insert a field everywhere that the user will be allowed to enter information. When you come to **protect** the form, the user will be allowed to enter only these fields, which remain unprotected.

Enter fields in the first 4 rows under the headings as follows.

- *Model* will be a text form field. The user will be able to type anything in this field. With the cursor in cell A2 (the first cell under **Model**), click the **Text Form Field** button. Double-click the inserted field (or select the **Form Field Options** box) and the following window opens:

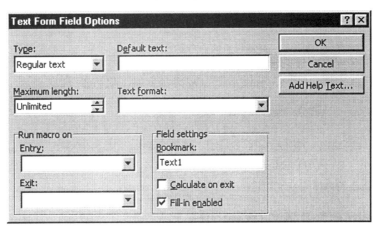

Figure 8.18: Inserting a text field

- The defaults can be left as they are. Make sure Fill-in Enabled is checked, to enable the user to make an entry in this field.

- You can add **Help** to any field. Click on **Add Help Text**, and the following window opens.

Figure 8.19: Adding Help to the Status bar

- Type the Help text *Insert Make and Processor speed*. This can either be automatically displayed in the Status bar when the user enters the field, or if you select the **Help Key (F1)** tab, the user can press F1 and the Help message will appear in a box. This is suitable for longer Help messages.

- Click **OK**, and **OK** in the Text Form Field Options box.

- In column 2 we will insert a drop-down list box. With the cursor in cell B2, click the **Drop-Down Form Field** button. The Drop-down Form Field Options window appears and you can add the items you want to the drop-down list, clicking **Add** after you type each one.

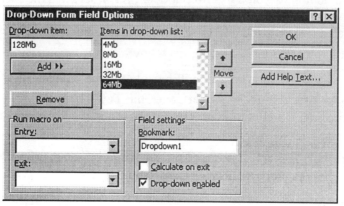

Figure 8.20: Drop-down form field options window

- You could add a similar type of field to the **Hard disk** column. We won't do that now.

- In the cell under **Speakers**, add a **Check Box Form Field**. No problems there.

Adding numeric and calculated fields

- Under **Price**, insert a **Text Form Field**. This time in the Options window (Figure 8.18) select **Number** in the Type box and select a suitable numeric format.

- Click the Calculate on Exit box. This will ensure that as soon as **Price** is entered, calculated fields such as **VAT** which depend on **Price** will be automatically calculated. Click **OK**.

- In the **VAT** we will insert a calculated field. Insert a **Text Form Field** and in the Options window (Figure 8.18) select **Calculated** in the Type box. Enter the formula $= E2 * 0.175$. (Remember that the cells are referenced A1, A2 etc in the first column, B1, B2 in the second column and so on.)

- Check Calculate on Exit. Choose a suitable numeric format and check **OK**.

- In the **Total** column enter another formula in the same way. The formula is $= E2 + F2$.

Protecting the form and entering data

It's time to try out the form. First of all you must protect it so that when you enter data you do not overwrite the fields you have inserted.

- Click the **Protect Form** button on the **Forms** toolbar. This puts you into data entry mode and you can now make entries in any field where **Fill-In** is **Enabled** in the form but nowhere else. Try making an entry for a 266MHz Pentium, 16Mb, Speakers, Price £1000.

- Unprotect the form to make any necessary changes.

Entering a conditional field

In the **Cash discount** column we'll enter a conditional field. There will be a 5% discount if the net price is £1000 or more, otherwise there will be no discount.

- Insert a **Text Form Field**, and in the **Options** window select **Calculation** in the Type box. In the formula box, delete the = sign and enter *IF E2 >= 1000 5 0* This means *If E2 is greater than or equal to 1000, discount = 5, else discount = 0.* (Leave spaces either side of *>=* and between numbers.)

- Set the numeric format equal to **Percentage**.

- Protect your form and try this out. It probably doesn't work – it doesn't on my computer anyway. *(Why not, Bill?)* To fix this, we need to insert a bookmark in the **Price** field. This is a way of giving a field a variable name.

- Unprotect your form again. Double-click in the **Price** field and in the Bookmark box, type *Price1*. Click **OK**.

- Double-click in the **Cash discount** field and instead of *E2* in the formula, type *Price1*.

- Protect the form and test it again – it should work this time.

Copying fields to other areas of the form

You can copy the fields from the first 4 columns to the cells below. The quickest way is to use the keyboard – Ctrl-C to copy a field, Ctrl-V to paste it. When copying the other columns you must adjust bookmarks and formulae – for example, the bookmarks can be defined as *Price2, Price3* and *Price4* in the other rows of the **Price** column.

Click the **Form Field Shading** button to get rid of the field shading – though you may prefer to leave fields shaded so the user can see what spaces they are expected to fill in. The shading won't print.

Saving the template and using it

Protect the form before saving it, and open a new document using the template to try it out. (Refer to Task 6.1, paragraph headed **Using a template stored on the A: drive** if you can't remember how to do this.)

Revisiting the Invoice

Now that you have had a look at the **Forms** toolbar, you may like to apply the techniques learned to the *ABInvoice* template. Inserting fields wherever the user enters data and protecting the form has obvious advantages. You can protect fields from accidental changes, and you can run macros on entry or exit from any field. You can insert a drop-down list field for different VAT rates or discounts, and look at other types of field that could be used.

For example, you could insert a text field at the bottom of the Invoice which says *'Click here to print the invoice'*. Then create the macro to print the invoice, and select it in the Run Macro On Entry box in the Text Form Field Options box. (See figure 8.18)

You wouldn't want this field to print, so you can make the text hidden as explained at the end of Chapter 11.

Chapter 9 - Mail Merge

What is mail merge?

Mail merge is the term used for merging a list of names and addresses with a standard letter to create personalised letters. It's a very useful technique whenever you want to send the same letter to several people – for example,

- to let customers know about a new product;
- to chase overdue invoices;
- to remind members to pay their club or magazine subscriptions;
- to send letters to all the people who send YOU junk mail asking to be removed from their mailing lists.

Task 9.1: Create personalised letters to customers

In this task you will:

- Create a *data source* (list of records) containing names and addresses of customers;
- Write a letter containing *merge fields* announcing a new product or service;
- Merge letter and data source to create a set of personalised letters.

Creating a data source

The first step is to put the names and addresses of all customers in a table.

- Open *Maindoc* and use your customised button to open a new blank letter using the *ABLetter* template. (If you have not got *Maindoc* handy, for the purposes of this exercise you can open a new document using the *Normal* template.)

- From the menu select **Tools, Mail Merge**. The following window is displayed.

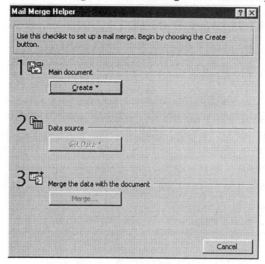

Figure 9.1: Mail Merge Helper

- Click **Create**, and on the drop-down list click **Form Letters**. A message pops up prompting you to select the location of your main document. Select **Active Window**.

- You are now returned to the Mail Merge Helper. Click **Get Data** and choose **Create Data Source**. The Create Data Source dialogue box appears as shown below.

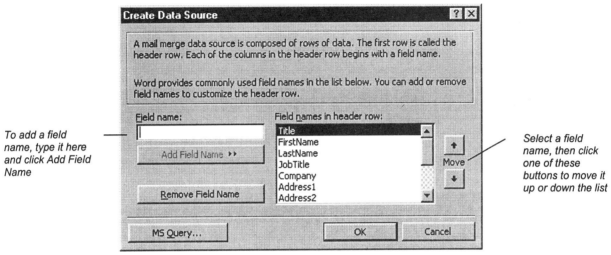

To add a field name, type it here and click Add Field Name

Select a field name, then click one of these buttons to move it up or down the list

Figure 9.2: Creating a data source

- Scroll down to *City*, click on it and click **Remove Field Name**. It then appears highlighted in the Field Name box.

- Change it to *Town* and click **Add Field Name**. *Town* gets added to the end of the list.

- With *Town* highlighted, click the Up arrow above Move to move the *Town* field up the list to appear under *Address2*.

- Now replace *State* with *County* in a similar way and move it up above *PostalCode*.

- Remove *Country*, and add a new field called *LetterSent* to the end of the list. This will be useful to identify who has already had a letter sent to them. Then, if new customers are added to the list, letters can be sent to just these customers by selecting records that don't have 'Yes' in *LetterSent*.

- Click **OK**, and the Save As dialogue box appears. Give your data source a name such as *Customer.doc* and save it.

- A new window appears:

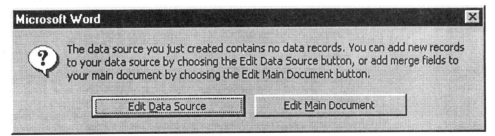

Figure 9.3: Another helpful Word message

- Click **Edit Data Source** and the data form pops up, as shown below.

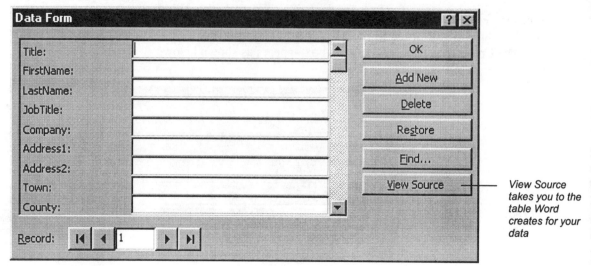

Figure 9.4: Entering data

Entering test data

You now need to enter about 6 records of test data. Choose your test data carefully to try out different aspects of the letter you will write later – what happens if the **Title**, **Town**, **County** or **Post Code** field is left blank, for example? The test data that you choose will need to be listed and included in your project.

- Enter the first record, using the Tab key to move from field to field. You don't have to fill in every field – in fact as mentioned above you should test out the consequences of leaving some of them blank.

- Click **Add New** to save the first record and move to the second record.

- Once you've added about 6 records, click **OK** in the data form and you'll be returned to the main document.

Note: If you click **View Source** in the Data Form window, you will see all your data in tabular form as in Figure 9.5. To return to the main document, select **Tools**, **Mail Merge** again. Then select **Main Document**, **Edit** from the Mail Merge Helper.

Title	FirstName	LastName	JobTitle	Company	Address1	Address2	Town	County	PostalCode	HomePhone
Miss	Jane	Shepherd			65 Ferdinand Avenue		Colchester	Essex	CO5 4ER	01267 567890
Mr	Bernard	Newcastle	Managing Director	Pearl Fishers Inc	53-57 Cliff Court	Felixstowe		Suffolk	IP7 5HB	

Figure 9.5: The data source in Table view

Creating the form letter

The next stage is to write the letter that is to be sent out to customers, inserting merge fields wherever appropriate.

- You should have a blank document displayed on screen with the Mail Merge toolbar displayed above it. When you click the **Insert Merge Field** button on the Mail Merge toolbar, a list of your field names appears as shown below.

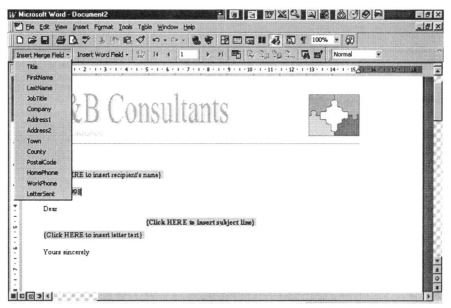

Figure 9.6: The Main Document screen in the mail merge

- To insert a merge field, click in the document where you want the first field inserted, then click **Insert Merge Field** and select the field from the drop-down list.

- Insert spaces, or press Enter whenever necessary. Your finished letter should look something like the one below.

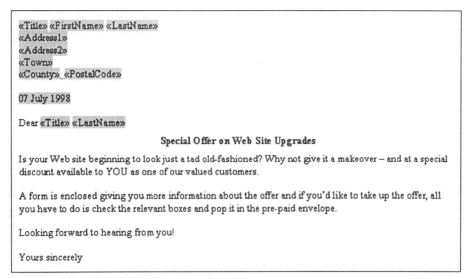

Figure 9.7: The main letter

- To view the letter with data in it, click the **View Merged Data** button on the Mail Merge toolbar to preview the merged document. The merge fields are replaced by the first record in the data source, as shown below.

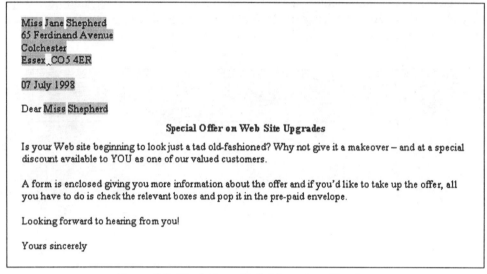

Figure 9.8: The letter with fields replaced by data

Note that letters should NOT begin 'Dear Miss Jane Shepherd' or 'Dear Jane Shepherd'. Either 'Dear Miss Shepherd' or more informally, 'Dear Jane' is acceptable. You will lose marks in your project for a letter containing errors in format, spelling and punctuation, so take care over it.

- The **View Merged Data** button is a toggle, so press it again to return to the main document.

- Save the document as *ABMerge.doc*.

Merging the data with the letter

- Select **Tools**, **Mail Merge** again.

- Click **Merge** and the following window appears:

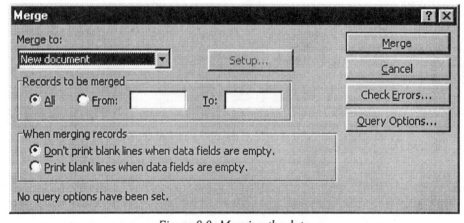

Figure 9.9: Merging the data

- The default is set to merge all records. The user could choose here to merge, for example, just records 5-6. For now, just click **Merge** to merge all the data.

- The letters with the names and addresses are shown on screen. You can now view them and print one or more letters.

- Notice that the letters themselves are given a default document name such as *Form Letters1*. You can save this document but you probably don't need to – the mail merge can be carried out again any time it is required. Close this document without saving.

Setting merge conditions

Frequently you don't want to send letters to everyone in the data set – you may want to mail only customers in Ipswich, customers whose invoices are overdue, or customers who have not already been mailed.

For example, suppose you have performed the mail merge as above, and over the next week or two you add some more potential customers to your mailing list to whom you want to send the same letter.

Or, supposing that once a week you look through your unpaid invoices and send a reminder to all customers who were invoiced over a month ago and still haven't paid. You don't want to repeatedly send the same reminder to the same customers week after week – so you need to be able to identify people who have already been mailed and exclude them from this week's mailing list. They can be removed from the list once they have paid up, or be identified as having paid, for example by setting a field called **Paid** in their record to 'Yes', or to the date when they paid.

Task 9.2: Send letters only to selected customers

In this task you will

- Set a 'flag' in each of the existing customers' records to indicate that they have been sent a letter;

- Add some new customers to the file;

- Set query options in the MailMerge Helper;

- Send letters only to customers who have not previously been mailed.

Setting a 'flag'

A *flag* is simply a field that you put a value in to indicate some condition or event. Earlier on we included a field called *LetterSent* in the record for each customer. Once the letter has been sent, we can set this to a suitable value – **y** for **yes** will do.

- Make sure the main document *ABMerge.doc* is open.

- Choose **Tools, Mail Merge** from the menu and under Data Source, select **Edit**. A popup box should appear listing your data source *Customer.doc*, as shown below.

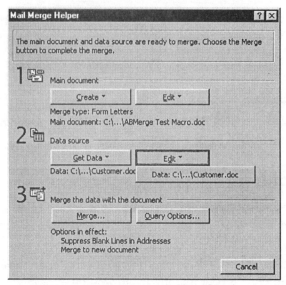

Figure 9.10: Editing the data source

- Click the data source (*C:\...\Customer.doc* or something similar) and the first record appears.

- Scroll down and click in the *LetterSent* field and type **y**.

- Click the **Next Record** button at the bottom of the window and edit each record in turn.

- Click **OK** to return to the main document.

Setting the query options

- With the main document on screen select **Tools**, **Mail Merge** again and select **Query Options**.

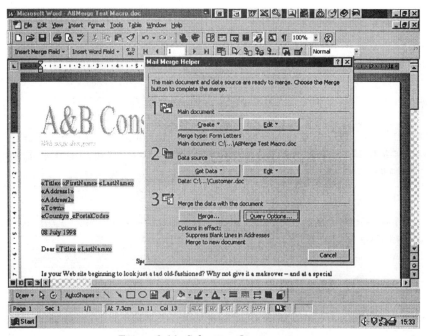

Figure 9.11: Selecting Query options

- The Query Options dialogue box is displayed. Select the *LetterSent* field from the drop-down list, **Not Equal To** for the Comparison, and type *y* in the third box as shown below. Click **OK**.

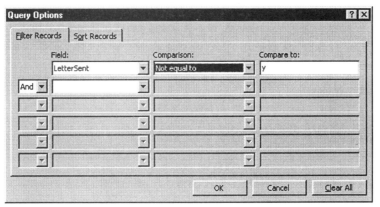

Figure 9.12: Setting the Query options

- Select **Merge** in the Mail Merge Helper window. Leave the defaults in the next window, and click **Merge**.

- You'll probably get an error message because none of your records fulfil the criteria you have set.

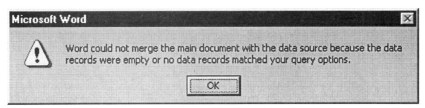

Figure 9.13

- Add a few new records, reset the query and try the merge again. You should find that only the new records have been merged.

Task 9.3: Send out club subscription reminders

In this task you will use conditional fields to vary the text of the letter sent out to different categories of club member. Senior members will be asked to pay an annual subscription of £20, and Junior members £10.

- Follow steps as in Task 9.1 to create a data source, or edit your existing data source as described at the end of this chapter. You need to have a field called *MemberType*, and you can delete or edit other field names as you think appropriate.

- Enter some test data, making sure you have at least one Junior and one Senior member.

- Create the form letter, inserting merge fields for the name and address as in Task 1. The text of the letter is shown below.

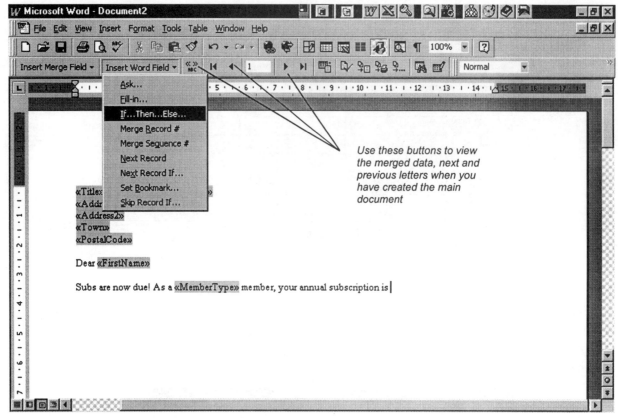

Figure 9.14: Creating a letter with an If..Then..Else field

- To insert the conditional field, click the **Insert Word Field** button as shown in the screen shot above. Select the **If..Then..Else** field.

- In the window fill in the Field Name, Comparison and alternative text strings. Different letters will then have different text at this point.

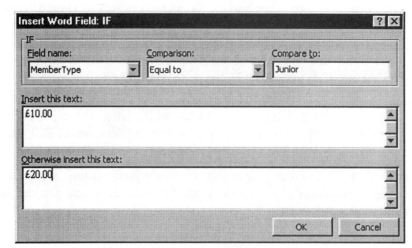

Figure 9.15: Inserting a conditional field

- You can browse through the letters as they will appear using the **View Merged Data**, **Next** and **Previous** buttons on the toolbar (see Figure 9.14.)

Displaying and editing field codes

You can display the field codes by highlighting (selecting) the field and pressing Shift-F9.

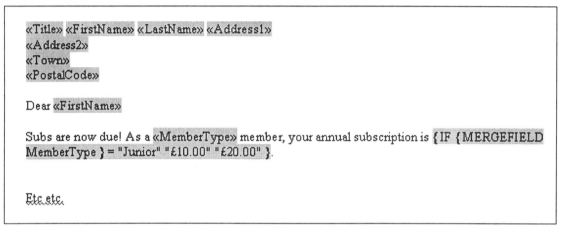

«Title» «FirstName» «LastName» «Address1»
«Address2»
«Town»
«PostalCode»

Dear «FirstName»

Subs are now due! As a «MemberType» member, your annual subscription is { IF { MERGEFIELD MemberType } = "Junior" "£10.00" "£20.00" }.

Etc etc.

Figure 9.16: Displaying field codes

You can edit the field directly when the field code is displayed. Try changing the subs to *£15* and *£30*.

Prompts to enter text

The **Fill-in** field will hold up the mail merge while you enter a specific value for each letter, or just for the first. You could, for example, have a Fill-in field for the date of the AGM.

- Add text to the letter: *The AGM this year will be held at 7.30pm on*

- Click on **Insert Word Field** and select **Fill-in**. A dialogue box appears.

- Enter a prompt *Enter the date of the AGM* and default Fill-in text: *Thursday 20th May*.

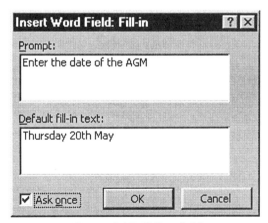

Figure 9.17: Fill-in field

- You'll be asked to enter the text again in the next dialogue box:

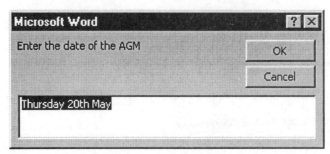

Figure 9.18: Entering the text for the Fill-in field

- Now try running the merge. You'll be prompted to enter the date of the AGM. If you checked the Ask Once box (see Figure 9.17) you won't be asked to enter the date for each individual letter.

Prompting for a different value for each member

Now suppose that you want to call each club member in for an audition (it's a drama club) and you want to specify a different audition time in each letter. The prompt needs to include the surname: for example, *Please enter the audition time for Shepherd.*

- Add text to your letter: *Please come for an audition on 19th May at .*

- Click on **Insert Word Field** and select **Fill-in**. In the dialogue box, enter a prompt *Please enter audition time for* and default Fill-in text: *6pm*. This time, don't check the Ask Once box. As before, you'll be asked to enter the text again.

- In the letter, press Shift-F9 to display the field code for the fill-in merge field:

  {FILLIN "Please enter audition time for " \d "6pm"}

- With the cursor positioned after the words "Please enter audition time for " click on **Insert Merge Field** and insert the LastName field. The field code will then appear as

  {FILLIN "Please enter audition time for {MERGEFIELD LastName}\d "6pm"}

  (You may need to click on *Shepherd* and press Shift-F9 to see the field code for *LastName*.)

- Now try running the merge. You'll be prompted to enter a time for each person in turn, for example *Please enter audition time for Shepherd.*

Editing the data source

If you find that you need to add new fields to the Data Source, you can do this easily.

- Select **Tools**, **Mail Merge** from the Main document.

- Select **Data Source**, **Edit** in the Mail Merge Helper.

- Select **View Data Source** from the Data Form window. (See Figure 9.4)

- Add or delete columns as required while in Table view.

- Save the document and select **Tools**, **Mail Merge** again. **Main Document**, **Edit** returns you to the Main document.

Internal and external data sources

In this chapter we have used an **internal data source** – in other words, the details of customers or club members were created in Word and stored as a Word document. Word also allows you to use an **external data source** – such as a table created in MS Access, for example. You simply specify the file you need as the Data source in the Mail Merge Helper dialogue box.

This feature is very useful if the user already has a database of customers and wants to be able to send letters to all or some of them. Although a Minor Project for the NEAB 'A' Level I.T. should not use more than one software package, it is perfectly acceptable to import an external data source.

Additional tasks

Look at other options in the Mail Merge. You can, for example, merge the data from just one or two specified records. (Look again at Figure 9.9.) Or, you can use a query to specify for example the surname of a single individual to whom you wish to send a letter. Alternatively, the Mail Merge toolbar has buttons to enable a user to quickly find the record containing a particular first name or surname, for example.

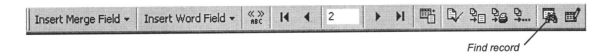

Figure 9.19: The Mail Merge toolbar

Pressing the **Find Record** button brings up a dialogue box:

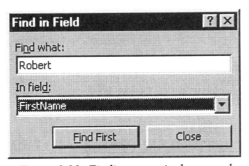

Figure 9.20: Finding a particular record

The record number indicator will display the appropriate record number so that the user can then elect to send the letter to just that person.

If you don't think the Mail Merge toolbar is particularly user-friendly, in the next chapter you'll learn how to create your own.

Consider whether these options would be useful to the user for whom you are developing your project.

Chapter 10 – Customising Menus and Toolbars

Introduction

(Word 7 users should turn to Chapter 17 instead of following Chapter 10.)

In Chapter 7 we had a brief look at how to put a new button on a toolbar. In this chapter we'll put a new menu on the menu bar and create a completely new toolbar.

Suppose that your user has three or four people that he or she regularly writes to – people like the company accountant, a major supplier, a co-author or partner. It's a nuisance to have to type in their name and address every time a letter has to be written. We'll automate the process so that all the user has to do is select a **Letters** option from the menu, and then pick the recipient from a drop-down list to open a new document with the name and address already entered.

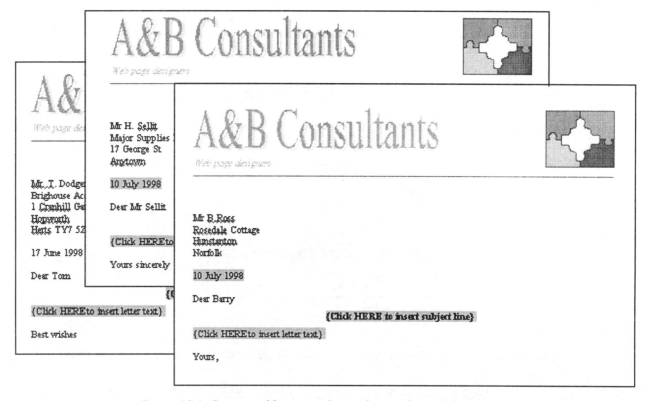

Figure 10.1: Customised letter template to frequently-mailed recipients

Task 10.1: Create a custom menu to open various letter templates

In this task you will first record macros to insert suitable text (e.g. names and addresses) in each of several letters, and then create a menu of options to run these macros.

Creating the customised templates

We need to record macros for each of the templates. Each macro will

- Open a new document based on the *ABLetter.dot* template. (If you are working on a network, you can try out the task in this chapter using the standard template *Normal.dot*. In your project, you should open a new document based on the specially created template that has the company letterhead already present.)
- Enter the recipient's name and address, greeting and closing lines.

The macros will be saved in **Documents based on ABNormal.dot**.

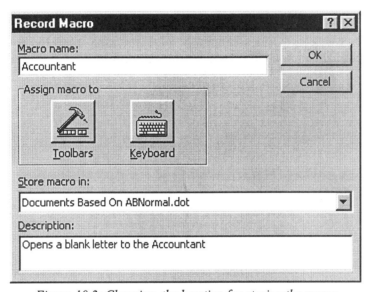

Figure 10.2: Choosing the location for storing the macro

- Open *Maindoc*.

- Select **Tools**, **Macro**, **Record New Macro**. Name the macro *Accountant*.

- Open a new document based on *ABLetter.dot* by selecting **Tools**, **Macro**, **Macros** and running the macro *OpenABLetter* which is stored in *ABNormal.dot*. (If you can't do this for any reason, just open a new blank document.)

- Type in the first recipient's name and address, greeting and closing line. This letter will be to the accountant. Note that you must use the keyboard arrow keys and not the mouse when recording a macro; clicking the mouse somewhere in the document cannot be recorded because the macro does not know where you are clicking relative to the current document. You can use Shift and the arrow keys to move in and out of fields.

- Leave the cursor positioned where the user will normally start typing.

- Stop the macro.

- Close the new document without saving.

- Repeat the above steps twice more, creating macros called *Supplier* and *Partner*.

Adding a custom menu

- Have the document *Maindoc* open on screen.

- Select **Tools**, **Customize** and then click the **Commands** tab.

- In the Categories box, click **New Menu** at the bottom of the list. Select *ABNormal.dot* in the Select In box.

- Drag **New Menu** from the Commands box to the menu bar next to **Help** (see Figure 10.3.)

- Right-click the new menu and type the name *Letters* in the **Name** box on the shortcut menu. Press Enter.

- To add a command to the custom menu, click **Letters** on the menu bar to display an empty box.

- Click **Macros** in the Categories box, and drag the *Accountant* macro to the empty box in the **Letters** menu. Click the right-hand mouse button and rename it **Accountant**.

- Drag the *Partner* macro into the box and rename it.

- Drag the *Supplier* macro into the box, and rename it.

- Close the window and test your new menu.

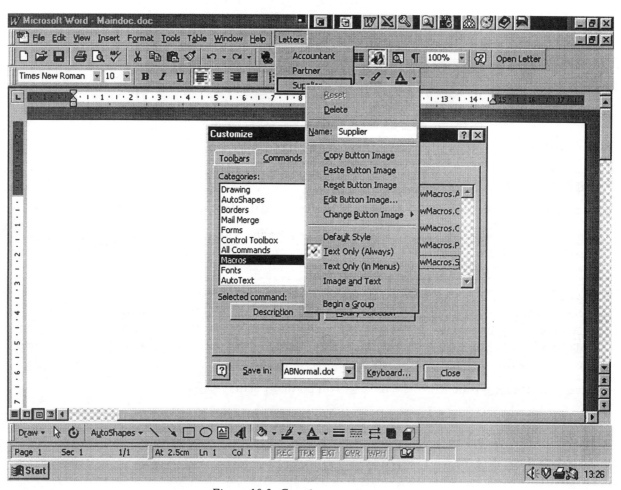

Figure 10.3: Creating a custom menu

Creating a toolbar

Instead of (or as well as) adding a new menu item, you could create your own customised toolbar which has a different button to open each letter – or to perform any other useful tasks, like printing business cards or With Compliment slips.

Task 10.2: Create a custom toolbar

In this task you will create a brand-new toolbar called **A&B Toolbar** which has options to print each of the three letters created in Task 10.1.

- On the **Tools** menu, click **Customize**, and then click the **Toolbars** tab.

- Click **New**.

- In the Toolbar Name box, type the name *A&B Toolbar*.

- In the Make Toolbar Available To box, click *Menudoc.doc*.

- To add a button to the toolbar, click the **Commands** tab. In the Categories box, select **Macros**. Drag the macros you want from the Commands box to the displayed toolbar, and name them in the same way as before, by clicking the right mouse button.

- When you have added all the buttons you want, click **Close**.

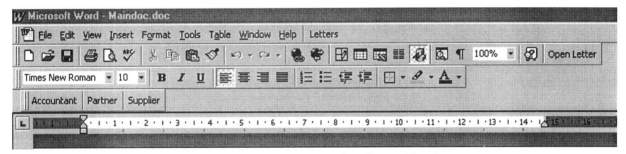

Figure 10.4: Custom menu and toolbar in Maindoc

Chapter 11 – Designing the User Interface

Designing the front end

(Word 7 users should turn to Chapter 18 instead of this chapter.)

So far you've created several types of documents and templates that would be useful to a user. Now it's time to review exactly what the user needs in the way of templates, mail-merge options and so on, and provide an easy way for each of these options to be accessed.

You could, for example:

- Create new menus on the menu bar;
- Create a customised toolbar with options for the user to choose from;
- Create a main menu of options on a special form, as shown in Figure 11.1;
- Use a combination of all of the above.

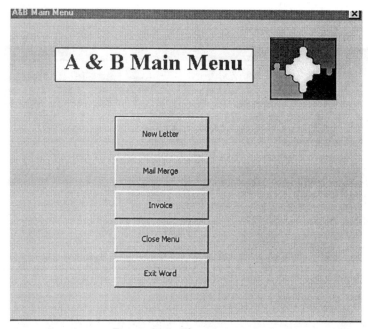

Figure 11.1: The main menu

How will the user access the menu?

Some thought needs to be given to how this menu will be displayed. For example, there is a subdirectory called Startup (Pathname *C:\Microsoft Office\Office\Startup.*) Any macros that are attached to templates placed in this directory will load up automatically. This is one way of getting a main menu to appear as soon as the user loads Word. Another way is to create an Autoexec macro to open *Maindoc* and the menu. Autoexec macros are discussed later in this chapter.

If you are using a school or college network you will not be able to put anything in the Startup directory, or create an Autoexec macro. You may also decide that the user will not necessarily want the customised front end to come up automatically every time Word is loaded – this is something that you would need to ask in an interview.

In this application, the user will start up the customised system by loading a Word document named *Maindoc.doc*. The menu associated with this document will have an extra item on it:

Figure 11.2

On clicking **Display Menu**, the menu form will be displayed, and the user can select the desired option. This way, the menu can be redisplayed whenever the user wants to select another option, whatever document is currently open.

Task 11.1: Add a front end to the application

Preparing the ground

Before we start the complicated stuff, you need to make sure you have at least one customised template saved which can be loaded by clicking a button on the main menu. We'll be using the *ABLetter.dot* template created in Chapter 6, but if you haven't got this handy, create a template quickly as follows:

1. Open a new document using the Normal template. From the menu bar, select **View, Header and Footer**.

2. In Times New Roman, 14 point Italic type the words

   ABLetter Template

4. Save the template on A:, naming it *ABLetter.dot*. If you don't use floppy disks, save it in your normal location, but be sure to give it the extension *.dot*.

The *ABLetter.dot* template will be the one that gets loaded from the customised menu. If and when you create a menu for your project you will of course be creating buttons to load your own customised templates.

Starting Visual Basic for Applications

Visual Basic is the programming language used in all the Office applications to create procedures to customise an application. Luckily you don't need to know much about programming to do some fairly clever things – you'll pick it up as you go along.

- First of all, open *Maindoc*.

- To get to the Visual Basic screen, select **Tools, Macro, Visual Basic Editor**. Alternatively, use the shortcut key, Alt-F11.

You'll see a screen similar to the following:

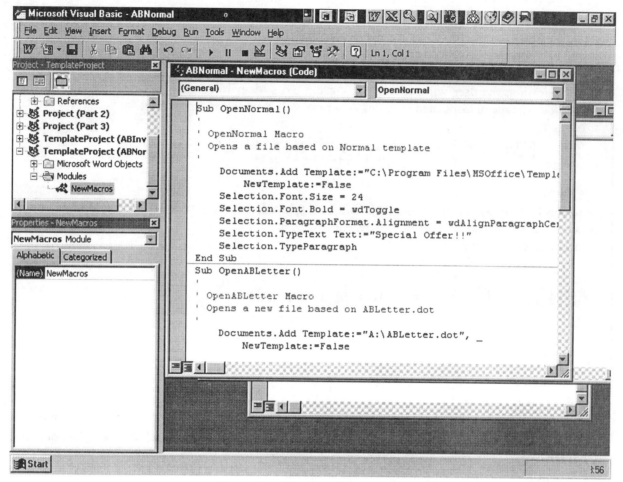

Figure 11.3: The Visual Basic screen

Note that:

- you now have a different set of menus along the top of the screen. You can get back to the old familiar Word screen at any time by pressing Alt-F11, which acts as a toggle between the two screens.

- The top left window is called the Project Explorer window and clicking on different objects in this window will cause them to be displayed. If the Project Explorer window is not displayed you can display it by selecting **Project Explorer** from the **View** menu.

- The other window visible is the Properties window. Properties are discussed over the page. Note that you can display the Properties window by selecting **Properties Window** from the **View** menu.

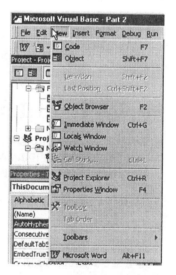

Inserting a form for the menu

- In the Project Explorer window, click **This Document** under **Project (Maindoc)**. This ensures that your form will be saved in the current document.

- From the Visual Basic menu bar, select **Insert, UserForm**. A blank form and toolbox appears on your screen:

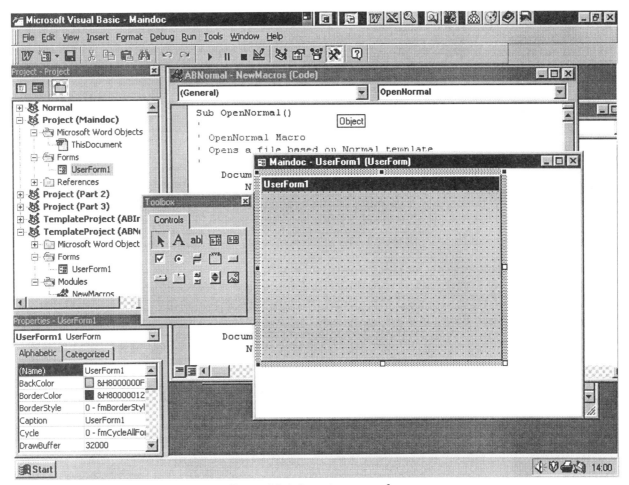

Figure 11.4: Inserting a user form

Visual Basic deals with *objects*. The form you have just created is an object, and any buttons, text or graphics that you place on the form are objects. Each object has a *property sheet* associated with it: the property sheet for the form you have just created is shown on the left-hand side of the screen. You can change any of these properties, like the name of the form, the background colour and the caption that appears at the top of the form (which is not necessarily the same as the name of the form).

- Double-click the name **UserForm1** in the property sheet. Change it to *MainMenu* (no spaces allowed in the name).

- Double-click the Caption **UserForm1**. Change it to *Main Menu*.

- If you like, change the background colour. (Select the **Palette** tab in the BackColor window.)

Adding text to the form

You can add a heading and a logo to the form.

If the toolbox is not displayed, click in the Document window or the form. If it still doesn't appear, select **View, Toolbox**.

- Select the **Label** tool from the Toolbox.

- Drag out a box near the top of the form.

- Change the **Name** property to *Title*, and the **Caption** to *A&B Main Menu*.

- Change the **Font** property to **Times New Roman, 18 point Bold**.

- Change **TextAlign** to *Centre*. (You may need to scroll down the Properties window to see this property – they are in alphabetical order.)

- Change **Border Style** and **Colour** if you wish.

Adding a graphic

You can add a graphic or logo to your menu.

- Click the **Image** tool.

- Drag a box of approximately the size you want on the form.

- Click the **Picture** property.

- Load a picture from, for example, *Program Files\MS Office\ClipArt\Popular\Jigsaw.wmf*

- Set the **Picture Size** mode to 1. Your form should look something like Figure 11.5.

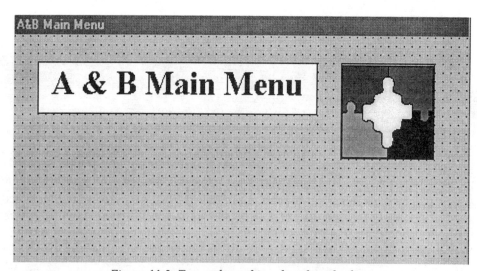

Figure 11.5: Text and graphics placed on the form

Placing a command button

The next stage is to place a command button which when clicked, will open a new document using the customised template of your choice – for example *ABLetter.dot*.

- Click the **Command** button icon and place a command button somewhere on the form.

- Change the button's **Name** property to *NewLetter*.

- Change the **Caption** property to *New Letter*.

Adding code to the command button

Now you're ready to add the VB code to the command button. The code that we need is the same as that for the macro *OpenABLetter* shown in Figure 7.6.

- Double-click the command button and the code window appears. Alternatively, you can switch between the code window and the object window (where your form is) by selecting **Code or Object** from the **View** menu.

- In the code window you'll see a procedure heading and ending:

```
Private Sub NewLetter_Click()

End Sub
```

- Just under the main heading, type the code as follows:

```
' Open ABLetter Template
Documents.Add Template:="A:\ ABLetter.dot ", NewTemplate:=False
```

- You can now try out your command button. Select **View**, **Object** from the menu and select your command button. Now run the code by pressing the **Run** symbol on the toolbar (Figure 11.6)

Run code

Figure 11.6: Running VB code

- What should happen is that a new document opens using your customised template. You'll probably have to move the menu out of the way to see the header. We really need the menu to close automatically as soon as a new document is opened. For now, close it using the close icon in the top right corner, close the new document, and return to the VB window by pressing Alt-F11.

- If you made any mistakes, you'll get an error message something like the one shown in Figure 11.7, and the code window will automatically be displayed with an indication of where the error lies. You're on your own here – you've just got to get it right! Note that the underscore at the end of a line indicates that the VB statement continues on to the next line. You can put it all on the same line instead:

```
Documents.Add Template:="A:\ ABLetter.dot ", NewTemplate:=False
```

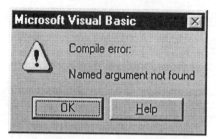

Figure 11.7: Error message

- If it all worked perfectly first time, select the command button and then select **View, Code** to display the code again. (If the code didn't work first time, edit and test it again until it works.)

- Add the following lines to the code to close the form after it opens the new document:

```
' Close the form
    MainMenu.Hide
```

- Test the code again, then close the new document and return to the Object window to display your form if you are not automatically returned to it.

Adding a button to close the form

Now you can add other command buttons as shown in Figure 11.8.

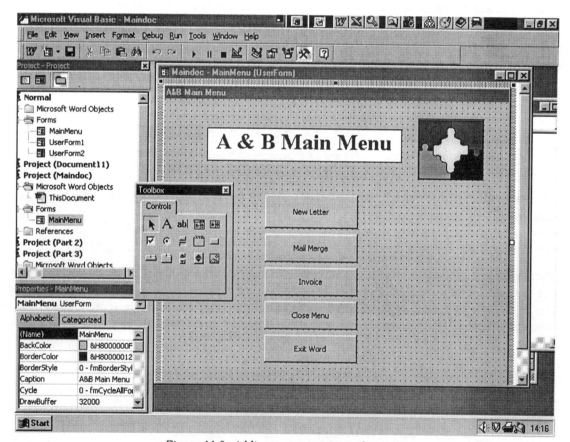

Figure 11.8: Adding more options to the menu

Adding code to the Mail Merge button

When the user clicks on the Mail Merge option they will be presented with the letter that was created in Chapter 9 (see Figure 9.7). They can then edit this letter or perform a selective mail merge using tools on the Mail Merge toolbar.

If you are not a whiz with VB code, the easiest way of writing it is to record a macro to do what you want and then cut and paste the code from the macro.

* Press Alt-F11 to return to *Maindoc*.

* Select **Tools, Macro, Record New Macro.**

* Save the macro in *Maindoc.doc*, and fill in a suitable description. Name the macro *ABMerge*.

* Select **File, Open** and open *ABMerge.doc*.

* Stop the macro.

* Close the mail merge letter without saving it and return to *Maindoc.doc*.

* Select **Tools, Macro, Macros**. Click on **Edit**.

* The VB window opens. There is probably a lot more code than you need displayed. The code you need is

```
Documents.Open Filename:="ABMerge.doc"
```

* Copy this code to the clipboard, along with the comment lines.

* In the Project Explorer window on the left, double-click on **MainMenu** to see your form on screen. Double-click the **Mail Merge** button.

* Paste the code from the clipboard.

* Select **View, Object** and try running your code by pressing the **Run** tool on the toolbar.

The code for the Invoices button will be very similar to that for the **New Letter** button, except that it will open the *Invoice.dot* template.

Adding code to the Close Menu button

The **Close** button simply closes the form.

* Double-click the button to open the code window. Under the procedure heading type the lines

```
Sub CloseMenu_Click()

' Close the form
    MainMenu.Hide
```

* Test out the procedure by returning to the form and selecting the **Run** icon from the toolbar. If all is well, nothing much appears to happen, and you will be returned to the form.

Opening the main menu

The next thing to think about is how the Main Menu is going to be opened in the first place. We're going to do the following:

  - Write a procedure to open the Main Menu.

- In *Maindoc.doc* we will put a customised button on the menu bar which when clicked will run this procedure.

Note that if you are developing an application at home or in an office on a standalone computer where you have full access rights to the Microsoft Office directories, you can save the procedure in a template in the *Microsoft Office\Office\StartUp* directory. It will then run automatically as soon as you load Word. As most students don't have full access rights to the necessary directories, we'll use a less automated but perfectly satisfactory alternative.

Writing a procedure to open the menu

The Project Explorer window needs to be visible in the VB screen. Make sure you are on the VB screen (press Alt-F11 from the document *Maindoc.doc* if you are starting a new session) and if the Project Explorer window is not visible, select it from the **View** menu.

- In the Projects Explorer window click on **Modules** in **TemplateProject(ABNormal***)*.

- Double-click on **New Macros**.

- From the menu bar select **Insert, Procedure** and name the procedure *MenuUp* in the popup window. Leave the other defaults as shown in Figure 11.9, and click **OK**.

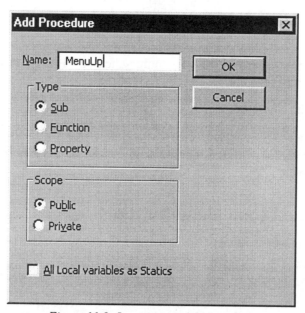

Figure 11.9: Inserting a new procedure

- A blank procedure will appear, and you need to insert one line as shown below:

```
Public Sub MenuUp()

        MainMenu.Show

End Sub
```

- Save the code by pressing Ctrl-S or selecting **File, Save Maindoc** from the menu.

- Return to the document window by pressing Alt-F11. You need to be in *Maindoc.doc* so close any other documents that you may have opened during testing.

Customising the toolbar

Now we're going to put a button on the toolbar that when clicked will open the menu. The menu will open automatically when Maindoc is loaded, but the user may close the menu and need to reopen it during a word processing session.

- Select **Tools, Customise**.

- In the window which appears, click the **Commands** tab and select **Macros**.

- In the Save In box at the bottom of the window, change the location to *Maindoc.doc*.

- Now drag the macro name **Project.NewMacros.MenuUp** on to the menu bar.

- With the window still open, right-click the button and you can change its name to **Display Menu**. Click on **Change Button Image** to add a picture.

- Close the window, save your changes, and try out the new button!

If it doesn't work, chances are the macros have been saved in the wrong place. Check Figure 11.4 and make sure your *MainMenu* is in Forms under **Project(Maindoc)**. If it isn't, drag its icon onto **Project(Maindoc)** in the Project Explorer window. To remove an object, right-click on it and select **Remove *Objectname*.** It may take you a few tries to get everything right but it's all good practice.

Adding code to the Exit Word button

You can record a macro in exactly the same way as for the Mail Merge button, edit the code and paste it into the button code. The code generated will be as follows:

```
Sub ExitWord()
'
' ExitWord Macro
' Exits Word
'
    Application.Quit
End Sub
```

Creating an AutoExec macro

You can create five macros that will run under certain conditions:

1. Any macro that you name *AutoExec* runs when you start Word.
2. Any macro that you name *AutoNew* runs when you create a new document.
3. Any macro that you name *AutoOpen* runs when you open a new document.
4. Any macro that you name *AutoClose* runs when you close a document.
5. Any macro that you name *AutoExit* runs when you exit Word.

AutoExec and *AutoExit* have to be stored in *Normal.dot*, but the others can be stored in any template. If you are working on a network, you will not be able to store the *AutoExec* macro in *Normal.dot*. Probably the best alternative for the purposes of demonstrating your project, is for the user to manually open *MainDoc* when starting a session. This will ensure that the customised template with all its macros, menus and toolbars is loaded. The user can press the **Display Menu** button to display the menu form.

If you install the system for a real user on a computer with no access restrictions, you can create an *AutoExec* macro, saved in *Normal.dot* which opens *MainDoc* and displays the menu form.

That's it for designing the front end. Finally, we'll look at a method of providing on-line help.

Providing the user with on-line help

You may want to include some on-line help for the user. One way of doing this is to create a separate Help file to accompany each document template, and then insert *Hyperlink* fields in the template which the user can click on to display the text in the Help file.

If you decide to provide on-line help, you need to plan out exactly where to place the '*Click here*' help messages and what text will be displayed when the user clicks to get help.

Task 11.2: Add on-line help to the ABInvoice template

In this task you will place two hyperlink fields in *ABInvoice.dot* as shown in Figure 11.10. When the user clicks on one of these, a Help message will be displayed.

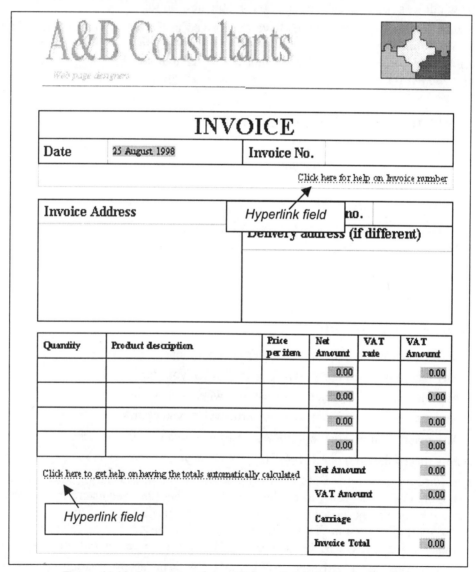

Figure 11.10: Invoice template with hyperlink fields for on-line help

Creating the Help file

The first step is to create a file which will contain the two Help messages which will appear when the user clicks one of the two hyperlink fields.

- Select **File, New** and open a new blank document.

- Save this file as *Invoice Help.doc* in your usual directory.

- Create the first help message. Type a heading and then the message, as follows:

Help on calculating fields
Click the Update button on the toolbar

- Press Enter twice and then insert a page break by pressing Ctrl-Enter.

- Type the heading and text for the second Help message:

Help on invoice numbers

Look at your last hard copy invoice or the last saved file name and increment by 1.

- Centre the text.

The messages are somewhat cryptic but you get the idea! If you click **View, Normal**, the messages should appear as in Figure 11.11. Switch back to **Page Layout** view before you continue.

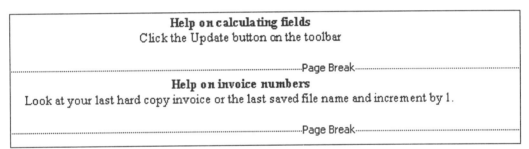

Figure 11.11: The Help messages

Next we need to insert bookmarks so that Word knows which Help message to display when one of the hyperlink fields in the Invoice is clicked.

- Select the first title, ***Help on calculating fields***.

- Select **Insert, Bookmark**. A window appears as in Figure 11.12.

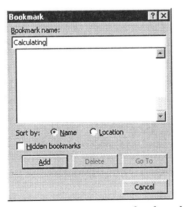

Figure 11.12: Inserting a bookmark

- In the Bookmark Name box enter *Calculating*. Click **Add**.

- Now select the second heading ***Help on invoice numbers*** and click **Insert, Bookmark**. Give this bookmark the name *InvoiceNumber* and click **Add**.

- Save and close the document *Invoice Help*.

Inserting the hyperlink fields in the invoice template

- Open the template *ABInvoice.dot*. (If you haven't got this handy, just open a new document for this exercise.)

- With the cursor in the bottom left cell of the invoice, type the text *Click here to get help on having the totals automatically calculated*. (See Figure 11.10.)

- Select the text (but be careful not to select the whole cell or you won't be able to do the next step).

- Click **Insert, Hyperlink**. If Hyperlink is greyed out it's because you selected the cell, not the text. The following window appears.

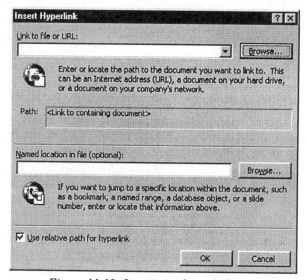

Figure 11.13: Inserting a hyperlink field

- In the Link to File or URL box, type *Invoice Help.doc* or click **Browse** to find the *Invoice Help* file in your directory.

- In the Named Location in File box, enter the name of the first bookmark, *Calculating*, or browse to find it. Click **OK**.

- Try clicking on the hyperlink field. The Help file opens and the message displays.

Adding command buttons to close Help

The user could now close the help file to return to the invoice. However, it would be more user-friendly to insert a button in the document near each help message that the user can click on, as in Figure 11.14.

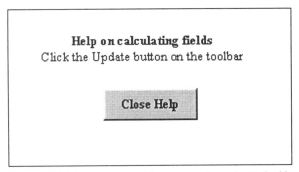

Figure 11.14: A command button to close the Help file

- Right-click anywhere in a toolbar and select **Control Toolbox**.

- Click on the **Command button** tool and place a button.

- Click the **Properties** tool to display the Properties box.

- Change the button name to *CloseHelp*, and the Caption to *Close Help*.

- Close the Properties box.

- Double-click your **Close Help** button to open the code window. Under the heading type the code as shown:

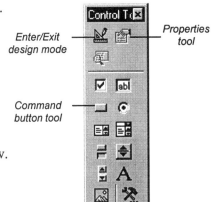

```
Private Sub CloseHelp_Click()
    'Close the active document
    ActiveDocument.Close
End Sub
```

- Press Alt-F11 to return to the document.

- Click the **Exit Design Mode** tool.

- Test your button. The file should close, leaving the Invoice template on screen.

Making the text hidden

You don't want the Help message to be printed, although you do want it to be visible on screen.

- Select the hyperlink text, and Choose **Format, Font**. In the Effects category, click **Hidden**. Click **OK**.

- If the Help text disappears completely, select **Tools, Options**. On the **View** tab check **Hidden Text**.

- On the **Print** tab make sure **Hidden Text** is not selected.

Additional tasks

Create an extra row in the invoice template and insert the other hypertext field. Insert another command button under the second Help message in the *Invoice Help* document.

Part 3

Advanced Skills in Word 6

In this section:

Chapter 12 – Headers and Footers

Introduction to Part 3

Part 3 is for those of you who will be using Word 6 to do your project work. If you are using Word 97, you can skip the whole of Part 3 and go on to Part 4. Part 3 contains exercises using the more advanced features of Word 6 which you will need to include in a Word project.

Word 7 falls somewhere between the two versions. Word 7 users should work through Part 2 but will sometimes be directed to the equivalent chapters in Part 3. (Check the logo in the right-hand margin.)

Working on a network with restricted access

Many students will be using a school or college network and will not have access to files stored on the server. This poses various complications because Word generally expects you to save templates and macros in default locations to which you will not have write access. For example you may not be able to:

- Save customised templates in the default Templates directory;

- Create and save macros in the default *Normal.dot* template;

- Create and save customised menus and toolbars in the default *Normal.dot* template.

The first thing you must do, therefore, is to create your own template on which all other templates and documents will be based. This template will be called *ABNormal.dot* and will be saved in your private directory on the *A:* drive or wherever you normally save your work.

If you don't know what a template is or why you should need one, don't worry; templates are covered in the next chapter. Just follow along for now.

Creating your own template

> **This is a very important step if you are working on a network!**

- Select **File**, **New** to open a new file as a template, by clicking the **Template** radio button in the New dialogue box.

- Without entering any text, click **File**, **Save**. In the Name box, type *A:\ABNormal*. (Substitute a different pathname if you usually save your work in a particular directory.)

- Click **File**, **Close** to close the template.

Every document that you create in the exercises which follow will be based on this template. This way, you avoid any problems caused by trying to save in forbidden directories.

If you are working at home on a standalone machine and have full access rights, you can use default templates and directories but you will not be able to transfer your work to a school or college network. Therefore you are recommended to create the template above as suggested.

Using headers and footers

A *header* is text or graphics that appears at the top of every page; a *footer* appears at the bottom of every page. A header is typically used to identify the section or chapter in a book, and the footer may contain the page number, a document identification of some kind, the author's name and so on.

Headers and footers are also useful when you are designing a letterhead for a club or company. The header can incorporate a logo and the organisation's name. The footer can include the company address (which could alternatively be placed in the header) and information such as the directors' names, VAT registration number and so on.

Figure 12.1: Headers and footers used in a letterhead

Task 12.1: Design letter stationery for a business

In this exercise you'll insert text and clipart into a header and footer to create a design for business stationery. You don't have to use the same Company name, address and logo – if you already have an end-user like a club or business in mind for your project, by all means use their details and your own artistic talent to come up with a good design for stationery. As part of the project, you could create a few different designs and show them to the end-user who can then choose one.

It will make life easier if you save your documents and templates using the same file names as the ones used in this book though, as many exercises require you to open a particular document and do some more work on it.

Inserting a header or footer

- Click **File, New** to open a new document. In the Template box, type *A:\ABNormal.dot* to use the template you have just created. (These instructions will always refer to *A:* as the pathname but substitute the appropriate pathname if you have used a different drive or directory.) This opens a new document based on the template *ABNormal*.

- From the **View** menu choose **Header and Footer**. Word switches you into Page Layout view if you are not already there, and displays a screen similar to the one shown below:

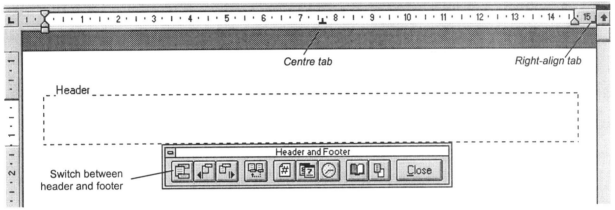

Figure 12.2: Inserting a header or footer

By default, you're placed in the Header area at the top of your current page. If you already have text in your document it will appear dimmed, in light-grey text.

The Header and Footer toolbar is displayed, with buttons to insert various items such as page number, date, time and so on. The only button you'll need for this chapter is the **Switch between header and footer** button.

Tip: You can also view and edit headers and footers by switching to Page Layout view and double-clicking the header or footer. The header or footer area will open.

By default, headers and footers are in Times New Roman, 12-point type. You can change this manually or by changing the header style as discussed in Chapter 2.

There are 2 default tab settings in the header and footer: a centre tab and a right-aligned tab. You can change these or add extra tabs as needed.

Inserting a heading

- Change the font size to **28 point**.

- Type *A & B Consultants*. Press Enter to go to a new line.

- Change the font to **10 point italic** and type *Web page designers*.

Inserting a clip art logo

To insert clip art, either from the selection that comes with Word or from your own CD:

- With the insertion point at the start of the new line under *Web page designers*, select **Insert, Picture** from the menu. You will see a window similar to the one shown in Figure 12.3.

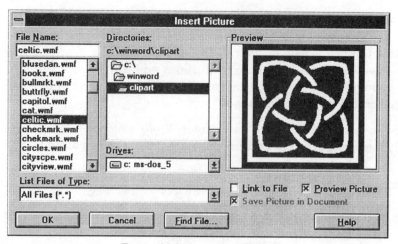

Figure 12.3: Inserting clip art

- Make sure the **Preview Picture** button is selected so that you can preview the clip art before selecting a suitable graphic. Click **OK** when you are happy with your choice. (I have chosen Celtic.)

- The graphic appears at the insertion point. You can size it as required by dragging a corner handle.

The graphic needs to be moved over to the right – you can select it and click the **Right Justify** tool on the Formatting toolbar, but this still doesn't give you the freedom to move it to exactly where you want it. To move the graphic freely it needs to have a frame inserted round it.

- If the Drawing toolbar is not displayed, display it now by clicking the **Drawing** button on the Standard toolbar.

- With the logo still selected, click the **Insert Frame** tool at the right hand end of the toolbar. A frame appears around the graphic and you can now move it wherever you want it.

- You can move any of the text around in the same way. Select it, frame it and then move it. If you end up with a border that you don't want, select **Format**, **Borders & Shading**, **None**.

- Use the **Line** tool to draw a line under the text. (Keep the Shift key down while you draw the line to ensure that it is horizontal.)

Working on the footer

Use the **Switch between header and footer** button in the Header and Footer toolbar to go to the footer. You can put the organisation's address, telephone number etc in the footer, or you may decide to keep the address in the header. It's up to you.

Press the **Close** button in the Headers and Footers toolbar to return to the main document. Save your document as *ABMaster.doc*, close it and bring it with you to the next session as you'll be working on it some more.

Additional tasks

Make a decision on which organisation you are going to develop your project for. If business stationery is one of their requirements you will need to find out exactly what information needs to go on the letterhead. Work on designs for other stationery for your chosen organisation such as a 'With Compliments' slip, a Fax header sheet or business cards.

Chapter 13 –Templates

What is a template?

A **template** is a preformatted document to which you add text of your own. The headed stationery that a school or college uses, or a blank invoice form, are examples of templates.

When you create a new Word document, you are asked on which template you want to base your document. At that point, you are offered the default choice of *Normal* and you probably just click **OK**.

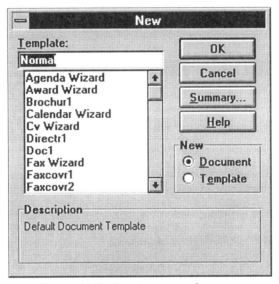

Figure 13.1: Opening a new document

However, Word also offers a range of other templates which contain preset information and styles for various different documents you might want to compose. For example, if you click on Faxcovr1, you will get a template suitable for creating your own Fax Cover sheet.

Notice that you have the choice of opening either a **Document** or a **Template**. If you want to use one of the templates to create your own letter, fax cover sheet or envelope, select **Document**. If you want to edit the actual template and save it under a different name as your own personalised template, choose **Template**.

Anything that you can put in a Word document can also be stored in a template. This includes:

- Text
- Graphics
- Macros
- Autotext (blocks of text that can be called up with a few keystrokes)
- Fields (e.g. current date)
- Font and paragraph formatting
- Styles
- Customised toolbars, menus and keyboard commands.

Creating a template

You can create a new template in several ways:

1. Select **File**, **New**, select an existing template, edit and save it. To edit an existing template, you must open it *as a template*, make the changes you want and then save it as a template (with a .dot extension) under the same or a different name.

2. Select **File**, **New**, select an existing template, open a new document and add all the boilerplate text and graphics that you want to appear in the template. Then save it as a template. (*Boilerplate* text is simply text that appears in every document based on the template, like a letterhead.)

3. A variation on the second method is to open any existing document, delete anything that you do not want to appear in the template, and save it with a *.dot* extension.

We'll try all these three methods, and you can then decide which to use for your project.

Task 13.1: Use and edit an existing template

This task has two parts to it. Firstly, you will use an existing template to write a letter as follows

-   Open a new document using one of Word's existing templates.
-   Try out the various features of the template.
-   Type a short letter using the template.
-   Save the letter as *Letter2.doc*, and close the document.

Secondly, you will edit the actual template, save it as a new template and then try it out, as follows:

-   Open the Word template *as a template*.
-   Customise it to your requirements.
-   Save it as *A:\ABTEMPL.DOT*.
-   Open a new document using the template and type a short letter.

Using the *Letter2.dot* template

-   Select **File**, **New** and select the *Letter2.dot* template. Click **OK** to open it as a document.

-   The template will appear on the screen as shown in Figure 13.2.

-   Click where indicated to type in a new company name and address, e.g. *A&B Consultants*.

-   Type the recipient's name and address, e.g. *Mrs J. Fergusson*.

-   Type a short letter in place of the existing text.

-   Type your name at the bottom of the letter. Delete any text you don't want such as *Typist's initials*.

-   Save the letter as *Letter2.doc* in your normal directory, and close it.

What you have just done is to use an existing template to create your own letter. However, you have not changed the actual template.

[COMPANY NAME]

[Street Address]
[City, State/Province Zip/Postal Code]

July 16, 1998

[Recipient Name]
[Address]
[City, State/Province Zip/Postal Code]

Dear [Recipient]:

[Type the body of your letter here]

Sincerely,

[Your name]
[Your position]

[Typist's initials]

Figure 13.2: The Letter2.dot template

Editing an existing template

The next stage is to customise the template so that you do not have to retype your own company name, address etc every time you want to type a letter.

- Select **File**, **New** and select the *Letter2* template again. This time, select **Template** before you click **OK**.

- The template will appear on the screen as shown in Figure 13.2.

- Click where indicated to type in a new company name and address.

- Edit the closing so that instead of *Sincerely* it reads *Yours sincerely* which sounds less American.

Creating a new text style

The template contains several different text styles. Click on various parts of the letter such as the opening, body and closing. Look in the **Style** box on the Formatting toolbar and you will see the style names **Salutation**, **Body text**, **Closing** and so on. Although the styles have different names they are all 11 point Arial. You could change them all to 12 point Times Roman, for example, if you wanted to. We'll just change one preset style here.

- After 'Dear *[Recipient]*' at the head of the letter, press Enter. Notice that the style automatically changes to one called **Subject Line, 11pt Arial, Bold, Italic**. When you write a business letter, it's normal practice to state the subject of the letter just under the greeting.

- Click on **Format**, **Style**, to bring up a list of styles in the template. With the **Subject Line** style highlighted, select **Modify**, **Format**, **Font**.

- Change the style to **Bold**, **Underlined** (not italic). Click **OK**.

- In the Modify Style dialogue box, select **Format**, **Paragraph** and select Alignment, **Centred**. Change the Spacing Before to *6* point. (See Figure 13.3.) Click **OK**.

- Check the Add to Template box in the Modify Style window and check **OK**.

- Click **Apply** in the Style box.

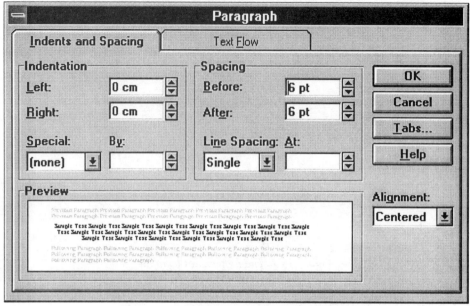

Figure 13.3: Changing paragraph attributes

- In the letter template, type *[Subject Line]* at the insertion point just under the greeting. It should appear in the modified Subject Line style.

Saving your template

When you select **File**, **Save** or **Save as**, Word automatically assumes you want to save your template in the default Template directory. The following window appears.

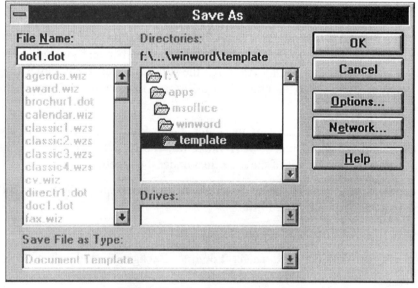

Figure 13.4: Saving a new template

- Enter a new file name, *ABTEMPL.dot*.

- Try clicking **OK**. If you are working at home, the new template will be saved in the Template directory. However, if you are working on a network at school or college, you cannot save anything in the Template directory, and you will probably get an error message such as the one shown in Figure 13.5.

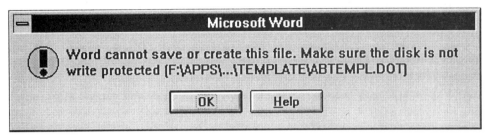

Figure 13.5: Word error message

- Click **OK**. You will have to type the pathname as well as the filename. Type, for example, *A:\ABTEMPL* in the Filename box. Click **OK**.

- Close your new template.

Using your template

- Select **File, New**.

- If you are working at home and have successfully saved the template in the default Template directory, specify *ABTEMPL.dot* as the template you wish to use. Click **OK**.

- If you are working on a network with restricted rights, you must type the pathname as well as the filename, as shown in Figure 13.6.

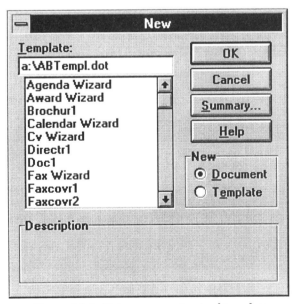

Figure 13.6: Using your customised template

- Type a short letter and save it as *ABLett2.doc*.

- Close the file.

We'll look now at the two other ways of creating a template.

Task 13.2: Create a template from an existing document

In this task you will create two templates:

3. A master template (*ABMaster.dot*) which will form the basis for all other templates such as the Business Letter template, Fax header sheet and Invoice.

4. A letter template (*ABLetter.dot*) which will contain boilerplate text and styles suitable for writing a business letter.

The first part is very quick:

- Open the document *ABMaster.doc* which you created in Chapter 12. It should look similar to Figure 12.1, though you may have used a different company name, address, logo etc. If you are in **Normal** view you won't be able to see the header and footer. Select **View**, **Page Layout** to switch views.

  (If you haven't created this document or have forgotten your disk, you need to go back to the beginning of Part 3 to create the *ABNormal.dot* template and *ABMaster.doc*.)

- Once you are happy with the header and footer, click **File**, **Save As** and save the file as a template named *A:\ABMaster.dot*.

  It's important to base all the templates around a single master template because later you will be storing macros and customised menus and toolbars in this template. Then they will be available to ALL templates and documents based on this one. All the macros and customised menus and toolbars in Part 3 will be stored in ABNormal.dot.

Now for the letter template. You need to have *ABMaster.dot* open as a template.

Inserting a date field

- Press Enter twice, and then select **Insert**, **Date and Time**. Select a suitable format for the date.

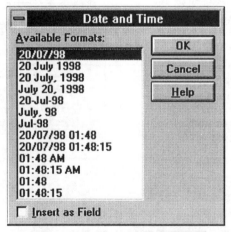

Figure 13.7: Inserting a date field

There is a problem with inserting the date using this method. If you check Insert as Field, then every time the document is opened, the date will be automatically updated to today's date. You want this to happen when you create the letter, but not when you load it up a week later to look at it. On the other hand, if you don't check Insert as Field, the date will always be displayed as the date you created this template.

The solution is to use a different type of field.

- Delete the date field you have just inserted.

- Click **Insert**, **Field**.

- In the Categories box, select **Date and Time**. In the Field Names box, select **CreateDate**. This will insert the date that a new document is created using this template, but it won't update it every time you reopen the document.

- Click Options and select *dd MMMM yyyy* or some other suitable format. This will display as, for example, 20 August 1998. Click Add to Field and then **OK**.

- The window should look like Figure 13.8. Click **OK**.

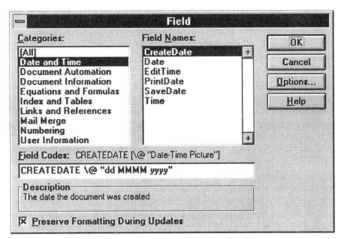

Figure 13.8: Alternative way of inserting a date field

- The user will have to press F9 to update the field to today's date when a new letter is written.

Adding a greeting, subject matter line, main body and closing

At this point you have a choice – you can create the letter template from scratch, entering for example *[Type recipient's name and address here]* or you can open your other template *ABTEMPL.dot* and copy and paste the parts that you want.

Note that if you cut and paste, the styles will be imported to your new template along with the text. You may want to change the style of the data to match the rest of the document.

The date is normally placed underneath the recipient's address in a business letter.

- Finally, place the cursor where the user would normally start typing.

- Select **File**, **Save As** to save your finished template as *ABLetter.dot*. Again, take note of where you save the template; Word expects you to save it in the Templates directory and you will have to type the path name to save it to your own directory.

- Close the file.

Summary

At this stage you should have three templates stored in a directory to which you have full access rights:

ABNormal - A blank template based on *Normal*.dot, the default Word template;

ABMaster - A template based on *ABNormal* containing the company header and footer;

ABLetter - A template based on *ABMaster*, containing boilerplate text for a business letter.

Attaching a different template to an active document

In Part 1 you created Business cards using the Normal template. If the *Buscards.doc* were to form part of your customised Word project, it would not display any custom toolbars or have access to macros and menus that you later create and save in *ABNormal.dot*. For it to do so, you need to attach the template *ABNormal* to *Buscards.doc*.

When you attach a template, you can use styles, AutoText entries, macros, custom toolbars, and shortcut keystrokes from the template. Boilerplate text and graphics from the attached template are not available, however. To gain access to these items, you can copy and paste them from the template or create a new document based on the template.

- Open *Buscards.doc*. If you have previously made the file Read Only Recommended, type in the password *modify* or whatever you chose.

- Select **File, Templates**.

- Click **Attach**, and then select *ABNormal.dot* from the A: drive or wherever you have saved it.

- Click **OK**.

Additional tasks

Create templates for your chosen organisation for their other stationery needs such as a Fax header sheet or Memo stationery mentioned in the last chapter. You should create them by opening the master template *ABMaster.dot*, making changes as needed and saving the new templates as, for example, *ABFax.dot*, *ABMemo.dot*.

Organise your work into different directories – one for your project work, one for exercises that you are doing separate from project work. Give careful thought to the naming of each file you save – a collection of files named *Letter1*, *Letter2* etc is an awful time waster, as a week later you will have to look through all of them to find the one you want. And while we're on the subject, LABEL YOUR FLOPPY DISKS with your own name, your course and a description of what the disk contains. You have absolutely no chance of ever seeing again an unnamed disk that you accidentally left in the disk drive in your rush for the door at the end of last week's lesson.

Don't forget to take REGULAR BACKUPS.

Chapter 14 – Macros

What is a macro?

A macro is a series of recorded instructions that you can run using a single keystroke or by clicking a customised button on the toolbar, for example. You can record and save the instructions, edit them and assign them to a keystroke or a button to automate tasks that you frequently perform.

In this chapter you'll learn how to record and run a macro, view and edit the WordBasic code that is automatically created, and attach the macro to a keystroke combination or customised button on the toolbar. **Word 7 users should follow the instructions in this chapter.**

Task 14.1: Create and edit a macro

Recording a macro

The first macro we will create will perform the following tasks:

3   Open a new document using the *Normal* template.

4   Display the heading '*Special Offer!!*' at the top of the page.

Before you record the macro you need to have a document open. Open a new document using the *ABNormal* template and save it as *MainDoc.doc*.

To record the macro:

- Select **Tools**, **Macro**.

- In the Macros Available In box, select *ABNormal.dot*.

- In the Macro window, click **Record**.

- In the Record Macro dialogue box which appears, name the macro *OpenNormal* and type in a description as shown in Figure 14.1. (Note that macro names must begin with a letter and cannot contain spaces. Use a combination of upper and lower case letters to make your macro names comprehensible.) Then click **OK**.

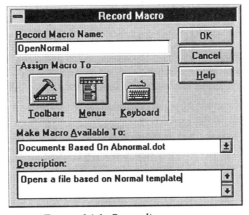

Figure 14.1: Recording a macro

Every keystroke you perform from now on will be recorded as part of the macro.

- Select **File, New.** Click **OK** to open a blank document based on the Normal template.

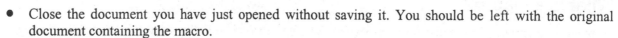

- In large, bold, centred text, type *Special Offer!!* and press Enter.

- Stop the macro.

Stop recording

- Close the document you have just opened without saving it. You should be left with the original document containing the macro.

- Save this document (*MainDoc.doc*).

Running a macro

Now you can try out the macro.

- Select **Tools, Macro.**

- Select *OpenNormal* in the dialogue box, and click on **Run**. A new document opens, and the text *Special Offer!!* appears.

You can close the new document without saving it.

Assigning a macro to a key combination

If you're going to use a particular macro often enough to be able to remember a keyboard shortcut for it, you can assign it to a key combination. You can either do this when you record the macro, by clicking on the **Keyboard** tab in the Record Macro box (see Figure 14.1) or later as follows:

- Select **Tools, Customize** from the main menu. The Customize window is displayed.

- Click the **Keyboard** tab, and in the Categories box, scroll down and select **Macros**. Select **ABNormal** in the Save Changes In box. In the Macros box select **OpenNormal**. (See Figure 14.2.)

- In the Press New Shortcut Key box press Alt *SO* (for Special Offer) and click **Assign**. Click **Close**.

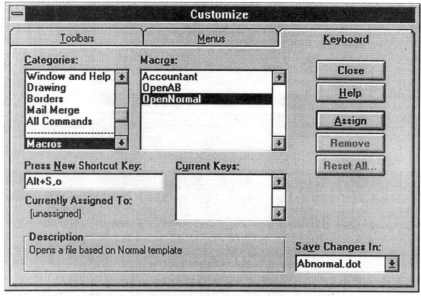

Figure 14.2: Assigning a key combination to a macro

- Try out your macro by pressing the shortcut key combination *Alt-SO*.

- Close the new document without saving it.

Editing a macro

In the last chapter we created and saved a template named *ABLetter.dot*. We're going to take the macro that we have just created and edit the code that was automatically produced to open a new document using the customised template *ABLetter.dot*.

- Select **Tools**, **Macro**.

- Select *OpenNormal* and click the **Edit** button. A new window appears as shown in Figure 14.3.

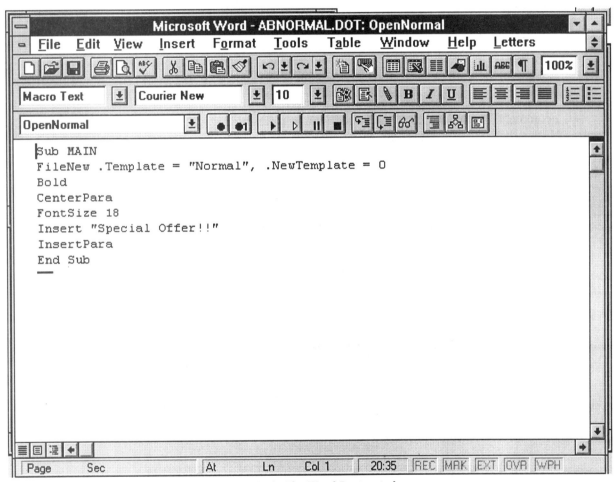

Figure 14.3: The Word Basic window

The code window is displayed. The language used is similar to Visual Basic but is not quite the same as that used in later versions of Word.

Note that:

1. A macro begins and ends with the lines

```
Sub MAIN

End Sub
```

2. The line
   ```
   FileNew.Template = "Normal", .NewTemplate=0
   ```
   is the command which opens a new document using the *Normal* template.

3. The remaining lines are the ones which set the font size etc, cause the text to be typed and the Enter character recorded so that a new paragraph is started.

We want to create another macro that opens a new document using the template *ABLetter.dot*.

- Copy to the clipboard the command shown in note 2 above which opens the new document. (Use **Edit, Copy** or your own favourite method.)

- Return to the document window by selecting **Window, Maindoc.doc** from the menu.

- Select **Tools, Macro**. Type a new macro name *OpenAB*.

- Type a new description *Opens a new file based on ABLetter.dot*.

- Press **Create**.

- Paste the contents of the clipboard to the new macro.

   Any line beginning with a single quote is a comment, and has no effect on the running of the macro. Comments are vital for documentation purposes and you should always include them.

- Add a comment line under the heading Sub Main, as follows:
   ```
   ' Open a new document based on ABLetter.dot
   ```

- Edit the line you pasted so that it reads
   ```
   FileNew.Template:="A:\ABLetter.dot", .NewTemplate=0
   ```
   (Substitute a different pathname if you are not using *A:*.)

- Select **File, Save Template**. You'll be asked if you wish to save changes to the macro *ABNormal.dot:OpenAB*. Click **Yes**.

Note: If you are working on a network with restricted rights, and you get an error message similar to the one shown below, you have probably tried to save the macro in the default template, Normal.dot. You will be given the chance to save in A:\ABNormal.dot in the next window.

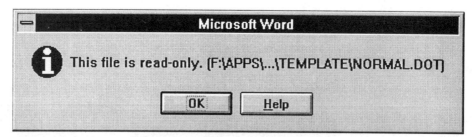

Figure 14.4: Network error message

- You get a message "Do you also want to save changes to the document template?" Click **Yes**.

- Try out the new macro from *MainDoc* by selecting **Tools, Macro, OpenAB, Run**. A blank document using your letter template should appear. (Select **View, Page Layout** to see the header and footer.) You can close this without saving it.

Task 14.2: Attach a macro to a button on the toolbar

You'll like this bit! We're going to create a customised button which the user can click to open a new document using the *ABLetter* template. Make sure you have *Maindoc.doc* open before you start.

- Right-click on the Formatting toolbar in a space between buttons.

- Select **Customize** from the popup menu. The Customise window appears as shown in Figure 14.5.

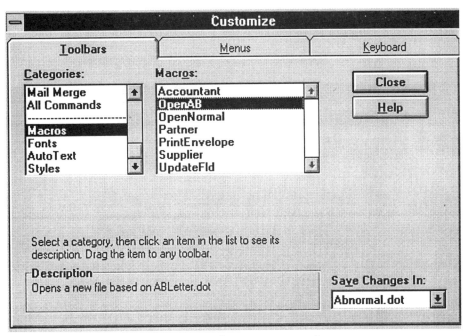

Figure 14.5: Attaching a macro to a button

- Click *ABNormal.dot* in the Save Changes In box.

- Drag the macro name *OpenAB* on to the toolbar. The other buttons will shift along to make room.

- The Custom Button window opens and you can assign either a picture or text to your button. Choose a suitable picture and press **Assign**.

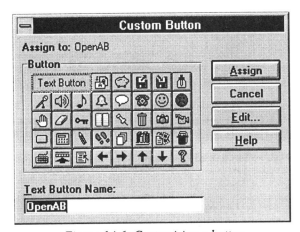

Figure 14.6: Customising a button

- Close the Customize window and try out your new button.

- Close the document that was opened by the macro without saving it, and then save *Maindoc.doc*.

More detail on customising toolbars and menus is given in Chapter 17.

Exiting Word

Try and exit Word now. If you are on a network and you get an error message like the one below, you have not been saving everything in *ABNormal.dot*. Try the exercise again and this time, save everything in *ABNormal.dot*.

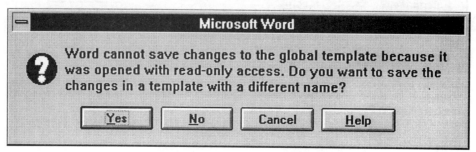

Figure 14.7: More network problems

Where is the button available?

The button will be available in all documents and templates based on *ABNormal.dot*. You won't see the button when you open a document based on the Normal template.

Task 14.3: Create a macro to print envelopes

When you've written a business letter, you obviously need an address on the envelope. There are basically three options:

1. Address the envelope by hand.
2. Use a window envelope and make sure the address is correctly positioned and the letter correctly folded.
3. Print the envelope.

The last option is a little tricky if you're using a network printer because the envelope has to be fed manually. However for a business user it is a useful thing to be able to do and Word makes it very easy.

Before creating the macro, try out the steps.

- Use your newly created button to open a new document using the customised template.

- Enter a name and address where indicated. You needn't bother writing a letter for the purposes of this exercise.

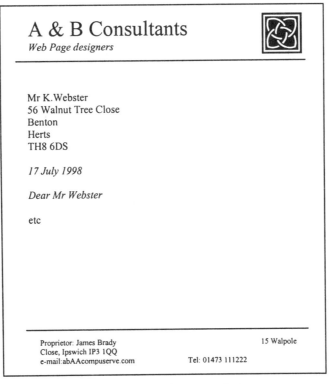

Figure 14.8: Using the letter template

- Select **Tools**, **Envelopes and Labels**.

- Select the Omit Return Address check box, as shown in Figure 14.9.

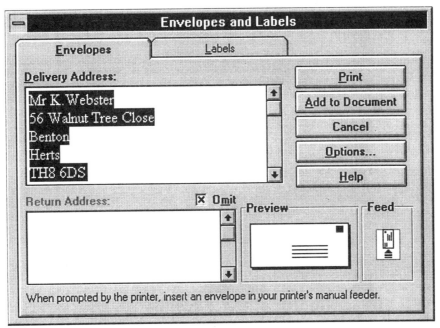

Figure 14.9: The Envelopes and Labels dialogue box

- You are instructed at the bottom of the window to put the envelopes into the correct tray. You may not be able to get this to work at school but it should be no problem at home, or for a user in an office.

- Once you have got all the steps to work, record them as a macro and attach them to another button on the toolbar.

Using the Organiser to copy macros

Word uses the **Organiser** to copy styles, macros, toolbars and menus from one template or document to another. When you work on your project, you may find you are developing the software on a school machine and then installing it on a standalone machine. You may need to copy macros from the *ABNormal* template to the *Normal* template, for example.

- On the **Tools** menu, select **Macro**.

- Click **Organiser**. A window similar to that shown in Figure 14.10 appears. If the templates that you wish to copy from or to are not shown, click a **Close File** button. The button changes to **Open File**. Click it and a list of all files appears, from which you can select your template.

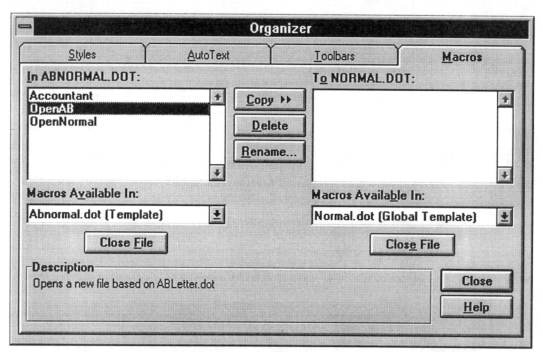

Figure 14.10: The Organiser

Don't forget to use the Help system if you get stuck on some aspect of macros or anything else, for that matter!

Chapter 15 – Tables, Formulae and Forms

Introduction to invoicing

Tables can be used in hundreds of different ways for all sorts of different applications. In this chapter we'll create an Invoice template which could be used to send out customised invoices for goods or services.

If you're going to do something similar for your project, you'll need to find out from the user what needs to go on the invoice. For example, if the annual turnover is greater than about £50,000 then the firm has to be registered for VAT and their VAT registration number needs to be displayed somewhere on the invoice. Find out the following:

- Is the firm VAT registered?
- Some goods such as books, are zero-rated, meaning that no VAT is payable. Will this firm be selling zero-rated or other goods, or a combination of both?
- Will the firm be charging for postage and packing?
- Are discounts given on any products?

You'll need to include the firm's name and address, the date, invoice number, the customer's order number, account number and address (and possibly a delivery address if this is different from the invoicing address), and details of the goods or services being invoiced. A possible layout is shown opposite.

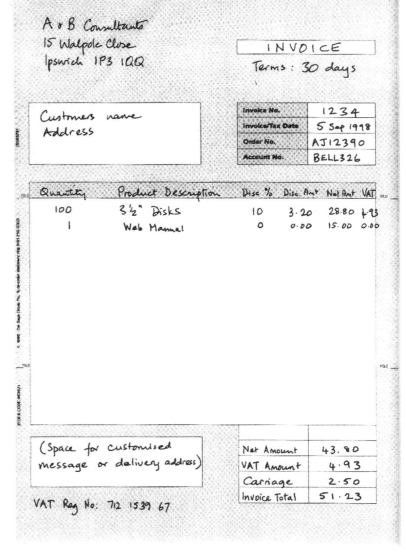

Figure 15.1: Invoice layout

There are hundreds of different ways of laying out an invoice so you need to consult your user, have a look at what is currently being used, and come up with a suitable design.

Task 15.1: Create a blank invoice from a table

This task involves creating a blank invoice form to the design shown below in Figure 15.2.

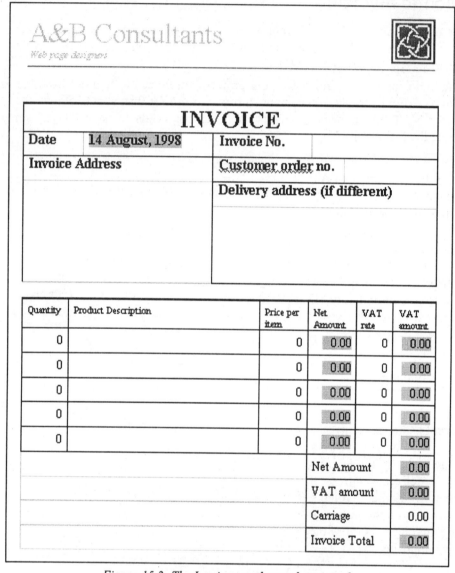

Quantity	Product Description		Price per item	Net Amount	VAT rate	VAT amount
0			0	0.00	0	0.00
0			0	0.00	0	0.00
0			0	0.00	0	0.00
0			0	0.00	0	0.00
0			0	0.00	0	0.00
				Net Amount		0.00
				VAT amount		0.00
				Carriage		0.00
				Invoice Total		0.00

Figure 15.2: The Invoice template to be created

Notes:

- *The footer containing the company address etc is not shown above but will be part of the invoice template;*
- *The user will delete the zeros in any unused rows of the invoice.*

Using the master template

It's a good idea for all the company's documents to have a consistent appearance, so we'll start with the master template and add boilerplate text to it to create a new invoice template.

- Load the template *ABMaster.dot* that was created in Chapter 13. This should contain just the company letterhead and footer.

- Save the template as *ABInvoic.dot*.

  (If you have not got this template handy, then load a new document using the *ABNormal* template, put a company name and address in the Header, and save it without closing it, as *ABInvoic.dot*.)

Inserting a table and adjusting row height

There are two ways of inserting a table. One is to click the Insert Table button and drag out the number of rows and columns that you want.

The second way is to choose **Table, Insert Table**. This is easier if you need more than about 6 rows.

- Select **Table, Insert Table** and specify a table of *6* columns and *12* rows, column width **Auto**.

  Note that if you have inserted the table on the very top line of your document, and you later decide you would like to insert a blank line above the table, you can do this by placing the cursor in the first cell and selecting **Table, Split Table**.

- With the cursor somewhere in the table, choose **Select Table** from the **Table** menu.

- From the **Table** menu select **Cell Height and Width**. In the dialogue box, set Height of Rows to Exactly **24 pt**. (Note that you can also set the cell height in centimetres if you want to. Setting the cell to an exact measurement means that the cell will not expand if the text is too long to fit, which means your table will always be exactly the size you have specified, but some text may not be visible.)

Borders

We can put a border round each cell in the table to start with, and then delete the borders that are not wanted.

- With the cursor somewhere in the table, select **Table, Select Table**.

- Select **Format, Borders and Shading**. The following window appears:

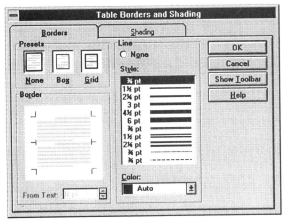

Figure 15.3: The Table Borders and Shading window

- Click on **Grid** to put a border round every cell and set Style to ¾ **pt**. Click **OK**.

Merging cells and splitting the table

The invoice that we are creating from a single table contains cells of different sizes. Also, the main body of the invoice is separated from the top half containing headings and addresses etc.

- With the cursor in the top row click on **Table, Select Row**.

- Select Table, **Merge Cells** to turn the whole top row into just one cell.

- With the cursor in the top row select the **Centre** text button, **Times New Roman 24pt Bold** and type the word *INVOICE*.

- In the second row, type the word *Date* in the first cell. Set the style to **Times New Roman 14pt Bold**.

- Select the second and third cells and select **Table, Merge Cells**.

- Type the words *Invoice No.* in the next cell. Set the style to **Times New Roman 14pt Bold**.

- Merge the fifth and sixth cells in that row.

- With the cursor in the third row, select **Table, Split Table**.

You can widen the cell containing the words **Invoice No.** by dragging its right hand boundary. Similarly, you can adjust the width of the cell containing the word **Date**.

At this point, your invoice should look like Figure 15.4.

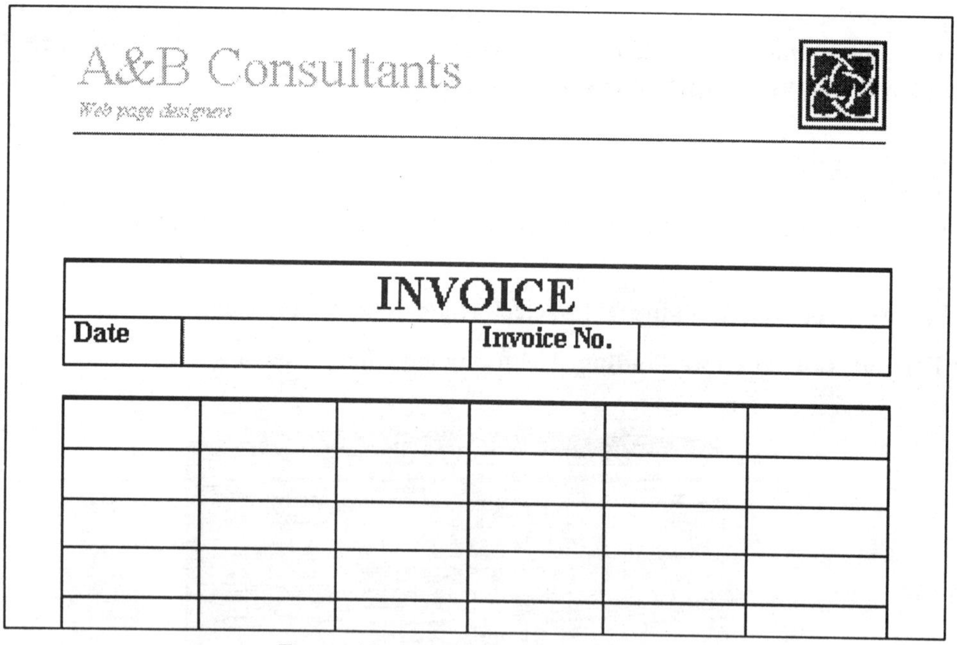

Figure 15.4: The invoice taking shape

Selecting cells, rows and columns

It is useful to be able to select individual cells in a table. You can then, for example, change the width of a single cell by dragging its borders, without affecting the rest of the column.

The Word Help system gives clear advice on this and many other topics. (Figure 15.5 was displayed using **Tables**, **Selecting Contents** from the **Help** Index.)

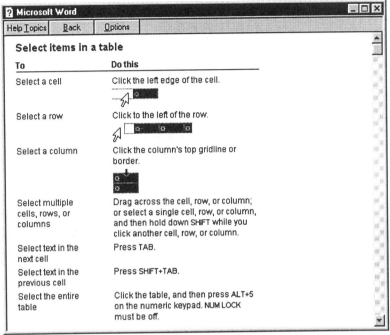

Figure 15.5: The Word Help system shows how to select areas in a table

Setting styles and individual cell borders

We'll use the same style, Times New Roman, Bold 14pt for all the rest of the headings. Set a style called **Invoice Hdg** by highlighting the word **Date**, typing *Invoice Hdg* over **Normal** in the style box and pressing Enter.

You can customise the borders around cells or throughout the entire table. We need to remove the borders to the right of **Date** and **Invoice No.**

• Select the cell containing **Date**, and select **Format, Borders and Shading**. In the Table Borders and Shading window (Figure 15.3), click on the right hand border in the diagram to remove it. Click **OK**.

• Select the cell containing the words **Invoice No.** and select **Edit, Repeat Borders and Shading**.

Now that you know the basics of merging cells, splitting the table, changing column widths and borders, edit your table until it appears as shown in Figure 15.6.

A new style named **Invoice10** using 10pt Times New Roman has been defined for the column headings.

INVOICE	
Date	**Invoice No.**

Invoice Address	**Customer order no.**
	Delivery address (if different)

Quantity	Product description	Price per item	Net Amount	VAT rate	VAT Amount

Figure 15.6: Changing widths of individual cells and columns

Inserting a default date

- With the cursor in the cell to the right of **Date**, select **Insert, Date and Time** and choose a suitable date format.

  Note: If you check the Insert as Field box, the current date will always be inserted in the invoice. Otherwise the user will have to insert today's date.

Inserting extra rows

We're going to need a few more rows, as the bottom part of the invoice will occupy 4 rows.

- With the cursor somewhere in the bottom part of the table, click the Insert Row button 4 times to insert four new rows. Alternatively, you can select four rows of the table, and then select **Insert Rows** from the **Table** menu.

Changing the alignment of text in each cell

- Type the text *Net Amount, VAT Amount, Carriage* and *Invoice Total* as shown in Figure 15.7.

- Merge the other cells in the last 4 rows and and remove the borders from the left hand corner cell.

- The text in the cells would look better if it was vertically centred in the cells. To do this, first select the 8 cells in the bottom right corner by dragging across them.

- Click the right hand mouse button and a menu appears as shown in Figure 15.7.

- Select **Paragraph** and set Alignment **Centred**.

- You can do the same for the rest of the table below the 'split' (i.e. starting with the row containing the headings **Quantity**, **Product Description**, etc)

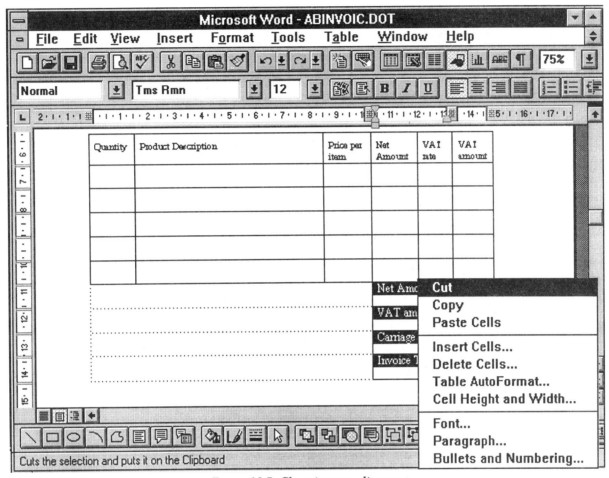

Figure 15.7: Changing text alignment

- Save your invoice template. We'll work on it some more in the next task.

Task 15.2: Enter formulae and test the invoice using test data

Test data

Look at the invoice now. The user will have to enter the information in the top part of the invoice, and also the **Quantity**, Product description, **Price per item** and **VAT rate** for each item. (Some items may attract VAT, others may be zero-rated.) We can enter formulae so that the Net and VAT amounts for each item are calculated automatically. The total **Net** and **VAT Amounts**, and the **Invoice Total**, will also be calculated automatically.

You need to make up some test data to test every part of the invoice. You need to calculate all the amounts manually so that you know whether or not you have entered the formulae correctly. This test data needs to be documented as part of your project.

Here is some sample test data for the invoice:

TEST DATA

Date: Today's date.   Invoice Number: 35

Invoice address: Mrs G. Bentham   Customer order no. 654321

                            5 Frederick Street   Delivery address:

                            Luton   8 Frederick Street

                            LU7 5RT   Luton

100 disks @ .32 each (17.5% VAT)

2 Manuals @ 27.50 each (0% VAT)

Carriage £2.50

Expected results: Net amount 32.00 + 55.00 = 87.00

                            VAT 5.60 on disks

                            Invoice total 95.10

Figure 15.8: Test data

The next stage is to enter the test data into the table.

- Enter the test data given above. Part of the invoice is shown in Figure 15.9.

Note: To get ½, set Num Lock on and press Alt-0189 on the numeric keypad.

Quantity	Product description	Price per item	Net Amount	VAT rate	VAT Amount
100	3 ½" disks	.32		17.5	
2	Web Manuals	27.50		0	

Figure 15.9: Test data entered into table

- You can immediately see that all these cells need to be formatted so that the data is centred vertically, so do this now, whether or not the cells contain data.

- Format all cells containing numbers so that they are right-justified, whether or not they currently contain any values. (Use the **Align-right** tool in the toolbar.)

We'll be entering formulae to calculate **Gross Amount** and **VAT Amount**, so leave the other cells blank.

Entering formulae

Formulae can be entered into a table in Word in much the same way as in a spreadsheet, although rather more clumsily. The cells are referenced as in a spreadsheet, as A1, A2, B1 etc., starting in the top left corner.

Figure 15.10 shows some of the cell references. In cell D2, for example, we want to enter the formula

$$= A2 * C2$$

and in cell F2, the formula $= (D2 * E2) / 100$

Qu A1	Product description		Price per item	D1	VAT rate	VAT Amount
10(A2	3 ½" disks	B2	C2	D2	E2	F2
2 A3	Web Manuals	B3	C3	D3	E3	F3

Figure 15.10: Cell references

- With the cursor in cell D2, select Formula from the **Table** menu. Delete the default formula and enter =*A2*C2*.

- Specify the number format as shown in Figure 15.11 and click **OK**.

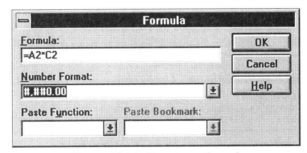

Figure 15.11: Entering a formula

- In cell F2 enter the formula = *(D2 * E2) / 100* and set the number format as above.

- Note that formulae in Word tables are always absolute, unlike in Excel, where you can enter relative references. You cannot therefore copy formulae to other cells and expect them automatically to adjust the cell references.

- Copy the contents of cell D2 to all the cells below it.

- You can toggle between the formula (field code) and the cell value by clicking in a cell with the right mouse button and selecting **Toggle Field Codes**. Do this now in cell D3.

- Alter the formula so that it references *A3* and *C3* instead of *A2* and *C2*. (See Figure 15.12)

- Toggle back to the normal view.

Quantity	Product Description	Price per item	Net Amount	VAI rate	VAI amount
100	3 1/2" disks	.32	{ =(A2* C2) \# "#,##0. 00" }	17.5	
2	Web Manuals	27.50	{ =(A3* C3) \# "#,##0. 00" }	0	

Figure 15.12: Viewing the field codes

- Click the cell with the right mouse button and select **Update Field,** or press the shortcut key F9.

- Edit the formula in cell D4 to read *=A4*C4.* When you press F9 to update the field, you will get an error message as shown in Figure 15.13 because cells A4 and C4 are empty.

*Note: You cannot insert field braces by typing characters on the keyboard. Fields are inserted when you use particular commands, such as the **Date** and **Time** command on the **Insert** menu, or when you press CtrlF9 and type the appropriate information between the field braces.*

Quantity	Product Description	Price per item	Net Amount	VAI rate	VAI amount
100	3 1/2" disks	.32	32.00	17.5	5.60
2	Web Manuals	27.50	55.00	0	0.00
			!**Error at A4**		

Figure 15.13: Error in formula caused by empty cell A4

- You will have to enter 0 in all cells which are referenced by formulae. (Look back at Figure 15.2.)

- Copy the formulae in the top row to all other relevant cells and edit them in the same way.

- In cell C7 for **Net Amount**, enter the formula *=Sum (D2:D6)* or an equivalent formula depending on how many rows you have got in your table. Select the correct number format.

- In the cell below this, against VAT Amount enter *=Sum(F2:F6)* and select the correct number format.

- Enter test data of *2.50* for **Carriage**.

- In the bottom cell enter the formula *=Sum(C7:C9)* and select the correct number format. (Note that since some of the cells have been merged in this row, the cells you want to reference are in the C column rather than the F column.)

- Select the whole table and press F9 to update all the fields.

The bottom part of the invoice should now look like Figure 15.14.

Quantity	Product Description	Price per item	Net Amount	VAT rate	VAT amount	
100	3 1/2" disks	.32	32.00	17.5	5.60	⎯ Cell F2
2	Web Manuals	27.50	55.00	0	0.00	
0		0	0.00	0	0.00	
0		0	0.00	0	0.00	
0		0	0.00	0	0.00	⎯ Cell F6
			Net Amount		87.00	⎯ Cell C7
			VAT amount		5.60	
			Carriage		2.50	
			Invoice Total		95.10	⎯ Cell C10

Figure 15.14: The invoice with formulae

Saving the invoice as a template

First of all, check that all the figures are correct (and your test plan will of course include some really thorough checking of every cell).

- Delete all the test data from the invoice (but do *not* delete the formulae).

- Insert zeros in all the numeric fields.

- The fields do not automatically update. Select the table, right-click and select **Update Field Codes** or press F9.

- Save the empty template as *A:\ABInvoic.dot*.

Task 15.3: Add a customised button to update all fields automatically

Using the techniques learned in the previous chapter you can now add a button to the toolbar which the user can press to automatically update all the fields on the invoice.

Recording a macro to update fields

- With the cursor somewhere in the table, select **Tools, Macro**. Give the macro a name *UpdateFld* and press **Record**. Type a description *Update all table fields* in the next dialogue box and press **OK**.

- Record the following steps:

  - In the menu click on **Table, Select Table**.

  - Press F9 to update fields.

- Stop the macro.

- You can examine the code created by the macro by selecting **Tools, Macro, Edit**.

- Add a comment or two to the code.

```
Sub MAIN

' Macro created by xxx on xx/xx/xx
' Macro updates all fields in the bottom part of the invoice

        TableselectTable
        UpdateFields
End Sub
```

- Return to the invoice by selecting **Window, ABInvoic.dot**.

Adding a button to update fields

- Right-click in the toolbar, and select **Customize**.

- In the dialogue box, select the **Commands** tab, then **Macros**.

- Drag the macro name on to the toolbar, and change its name to *Update Fields*. Click **Assign**.

- Close the Customize window, and save the template.

- Enter some test data and note that the fields do not automatically update.

- Press your new **Update Fields** button. Hey presto!

The manual processes involved

In your project work, you must consider HOW the user will use an invoice template such as the one you have created, and document this in the user manual. For example, the user may print out two copies of each invoice, one to send to the customer and one to keep in a file near at hand. When a new invoice is to be printed, the user can load the template, look up the last Invoice number used and enter the next number. The invoice can be saved as *Invoice147.doc* or whatever number it was, in a special Invoices directory. When the customer pays the invoice, the user can handwrite, for example, **Paid 12/09/98** on the invoice, and that way, keep track of who has not yet paid and send reminders for overdue invoices.

Such a system is really only suitable for a business sending out a small number of invoices – for more than about 3 invoices a week, I would recommend an Accounts system such as Sage Sterling for Windows!

Using Word to create a form

You have just created a template for an invoice, and have seen how to insert a formula into a cell. However there are many other types of form that Word can help you to create, such as:

- An online order form;
- A multiple choice test or questionnaire;
- An application or enrolment form for a college course.

The first step in creating a form is to create a template containing all the basic information that is to go on the form, and any list boxes, check boxes, dialog boxes and Help features you want to include. The template may also contain Autotext entries and macros. You can then protect the areas of the form that you don't want a user to be able to change.

Task 15.4: Create a form to advertise special offers

In this task you will create a form which the user can fill in and print each week to advertise special offers on computers. The form when printed will look something like Figure 15.15.

This week's bargains

Model	Memory	Hard Disk	Speakers	Price	VAT	Total	Cash Discount
Tiny Pentium 266	8Mb	2GB	☒	£1,000.00	£175.00	1175.00	5%
Time 486	4Mb	1GB	☐	£600.00	£105.00	705.00	0%
Vector Pentium 166	16Mb	4Gb	☒	£999.00	£174.82	1173.82	0%
Time Pentium 300	32Mb	4Gb	☒	£1,350.00	£236.25	1586.25	5%

Figure 15.15: The printed form

Many forms are based around a table.

- Open the template *ABMaster.dot* and save it as *ABForm.dot*.

- Type the heading *This week's bargains* as in Figure 15.15.

- Insert a table of 8 columns and 5 rows.

- Type the headings as shown in Figure 15.15 and shade the top row.

The Forms toolbar

Word has a special toolbar which enables you to insert different types of field anywhere on a form, set various properties and protect the form.

- Right-click the mouse on a toolbar and select **Forms** (or select **View, Toolbars, Forms**).
  The Forms toolbar appears as shown in Figure 15.16.

Figure 15.16: The Forms toolbar

When you create a form template, you must insert a field everywhere that the user will be allowed to enter information. When you come to **protect** the form, the user will only be allowed to enter these fields, which remain unprotected.

Enter fields in the first 4 rows under the headings as follows.

- *Model* will be a text form field. The user will be able to type anything in this field. With the cursor in cell A2 (the first cell under **Model**), click the **Text Form Field** button. Double-click the inserted field (or select the **Form Field Options** box) and the following window opens:

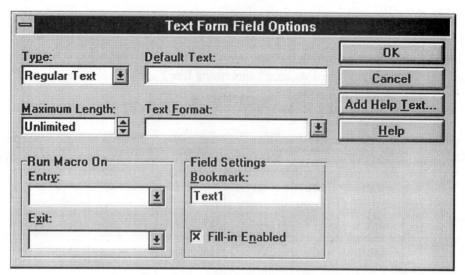

Figure 15.17: Inserting a text field

- The defaults can be left as they are. Make sure Fill-in Enabled is checked, to enable the user to make an entry in this field.

- You can add **Help** to any field. Click on **Add Help Text**, and the following window opens.

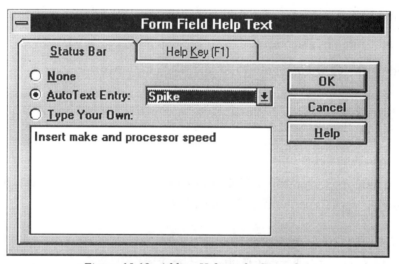

Figure 15.18: Adding Help to the Status bar

- Type the Help text *Insert make and processor speed*. This can either be automatically displayed in the Status bar when the user enters the field, or if you select the **Help Key (F1)** tab, the user can press F1 and the Help message will appear in a box. This is suitable for longer Help messages.

- Click **OK**, and **OK** in the Text Form Field options box.

- In column 2 we will insert a drop-down list box. With the cursor in cell B2, click the **Drop-Down Form Field** button. The **Drop-down Form Field Options** window appears and you can add the items you want to the drop-down list, clicking **Add** after you type each one.

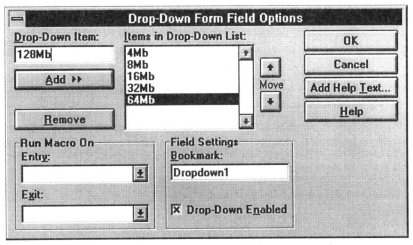

Figure 15.19: Drop-down form field options window

- You could add a similar type of field to the **Hard disk** column. We won't do that now.

- In the cell under **Speakers**, add a **Check Box Form Field**. No problems there.

Adding numeric and calculated fields

- Under **Price**, insert a **Text Form Field**. This time in the Options window (Figure 8.18) select **Number** in the Type box and select a suitable numeric format.

- Click the Calculate on Exit box. This will ensure that as soon as **Price** is entered, calculated fields such as **VAT** which depend on **Price** will be automatically calculated. Click **OK**.

- In the **VAT** column we will insert a calculated field. Insert a **Text Form Field** and in the Options window (Figure 8.18) select **Calculated** in the Type box. Enter the formula = *E2 * 0.175*. (Remember that the cells are referenced A1, A2 etc in the first column, B1, B2 in the second column and so on.)

- Choose a suitable numeric format and check **OK**.

- In the **Total** column enter another formula in the same way. The formula is = *E2 + F2.*

Protecting the form and entering data

It's time to try out the form. First of all you must protect it so that when you enter data you don't overwrite your fields.

- Click the **Protect Form** button on the **Forms** toolbar. This puts you into data entry mode and you can now make entries in any field where **Fill-in** is **Enabled** in the form but nowhere else. Try making an entry for a 266MHz Pentium, 16Mb, Speakers, Price £1000.

- The fields for **VAT** and **Total** do not automatically update. Unprotect the form, then click in each calculated field and press F9 to update it.

  It would be desirable to get these fields to update automatically as soon as **Price** is entered – we'll do that after entering the next field, which will also need automatically updating.

- Leave the form unprotected to make any necessary changes.

Entering a conditional field

In the **Cash discount** column we'll enter a conditional field. There will be a 5% discount if the net price is £1000 or more, otherwise there will be no discount.

- Insert a **Text Form Field**, and in the **Options** window select **Calculation** in the Type box. In the formula box, delete the = sign and enter *IF E2 >= 1000 5 0* This means *'If E2 is greater than or equal to 1000, discount = 5, else discount = 0.* (Leave spaces either side of >= and between numbers.)

- Set the numeric format equal to percentage.

- Protect your form and enter a price to try this out. Then unprotect the form and update each calculated field by pressing F9. The conditional field probably doesn't work – it doesn't on my computer anyway. To fix this, we need to insert a bookmark in the **Price** field. This is a way of giving a field a variable name.

- Unprotect your form again. Double-click in the **Price** field and in the Bookmark box, type *Price1*. Click **OK**.

- Double-click in the **Cash discount** field and instead of *E2* in the formula, type *Price1*.

- Protect the form and test it again – it should work this time.

Running a macro on entry or exit

As soon as the user exits the **Price** field, the fields for **VAT**, **Total** and **Cash Discount** need to update automatically. We need to write a macro that will be run on exit from the **Price** field.

- Unprotect the form.

- With the cursor in the Price field, select **Tools, Macro, Record**.

- Give the macro the name *CalcFields*. Make it available in **ABForm.dot**, and type in a suitable description. Click **OK**.

- The macro is now recording. Press the Tab key (remember, you can't use the mouse to move around when recording a macro) and press F9 to update the **VAT** field.

- Repeat twice more to update the fields for **Total** and **Cash Discount**.

- Stop the macro.

- Double-click the Price field to display the Text Form Field Options box.

- In the Run Macro On Exit box, select **CalcFields**. Click **OK**.

- Protect the form again and test it.

Copying fields to other areas of the form

You can copy the fields from the first 4 columns to the cells below. The quickest way is to use the keyboard – Ctrl-C to copy a field, Ctrl-V to paste it. When copying the other columns you must adjust bookmarks and formulae – for example, the bookmarks can be defined as *Price2, Price3* and *Price4* in the other rows of the **Price** column.

Click the **Form Field Shading** button to get rid of the field shading – though you may prefer to leave fields shaded so the user can see what spaces they are expected to fill in. The shading won't print.

Saving the template and using it

Protect the form before saving it, and open a new document using the template to try it out.

Revisiting the Invoice

Now that you have had a look at the **Forms** toolbar, you may like to apply the techniques learned to the *ABInvoic* template. Inserting fields wherever the user enters data and protecting the form has obvious advantages. You can protect fields from accidental changes, and you can run macros on entry or exit from any field.

For example, you could insert a text field at the bottom of the Invoice which says *'Click here to print the invoice'*. Then create the macro to print the invoice, and select it in the Run Macro On Entry box in the Text Form Field Options box. (See figure 15.17)

You wouldn't want this field to print, so you can make the text hidden as explained at the end of Chapter 11.

Chapter 16 - Mail Merge

What is mail merge?

Mail merge is the term used for merging a list of names and addresses with a standard letter to create personalised letters. It's a very useful technique whenever you want to send the same letter to several people – for example,

- to let customers know about a new product;
- to chase overdue invoices;
- to remind members to pay their club or magazine subscriptions;
- to send letters to all the people who send YOU junk mail asking to be removed from their mailing lists.

Task 16.1: Create personalised letters to customers

In this task you will:

- Create a *data source* (list of records) containing names and addresses of customers;
- Write a letter containing *merge fields* announcing a new product or service;
- Merge letter and data source to create a set of personalised letters.

Creating a data source

The first step is to put the names and addresses of all customers in a table.

- Open a new blank document, using the *ABLetter* or *Normal* template.
- From the menu select **Tools**, **Mail Merge**. The following window is displayed.

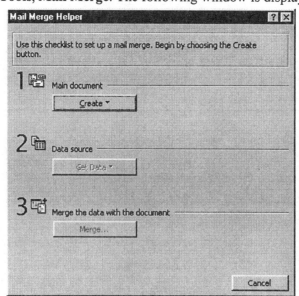

Figure 16.1: Mail Merge Helper

- Click **Create**, and in the drop-down list choose **Form Letters**. A message pops up prompting you to select the location of your main document. Select **Active Window**.

- You are now returned to the Mail Merge Helper. Click **Get Data** and choose **Create Data Source**. The Create Data Source dialogue box appears as shown below.

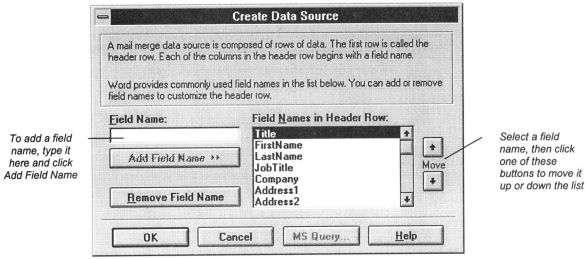

Figure 16.2: Creating a data source

- Scroll down to *City*, click on it and click **Remove Field Name**. It then appears highlighted in the Field Name box.

- Change it to *Town* and click Add Field Name. *Town* gets added to the end of the list.

- With *Town* highlighted, click the Up arrow above **Move** to move the *Town* field up the list to appear under *Address2*.

- Now replace *State* with *County* in a similar way and move it up above *PostalCode*.

- Remove *Country*, and add a new field called *LetterSent* to the end of the list. This will be useful to identify who has already had a letter sent to them. Then, if new customers are added to the list, letters can be sent to just these customers by selecting records that don't have **Yes** in *LetterSent*.

- Click **OK**, and the Save Data Source dialogue box appears. Give your data source a name such as *Customer.doc* and save it.

- A new window appears as shown below:

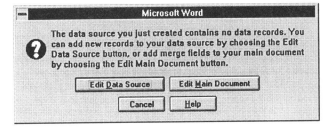

Figure 16.3: Another helpful Word message

147

- Click **Edit Data Source** and the data form pops up, as shown below.

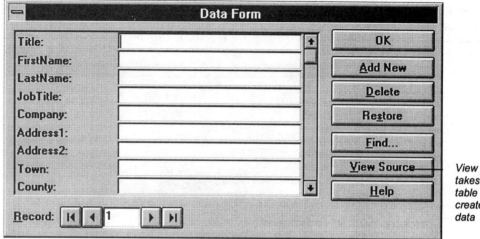

Figure 16.4: Entering data

Entering test data

You now need to enter about 6 records of test data. Choose your test data carefully to try out different aspects of the letter you will write later – what happens if the Title, Town, County or Post Code field is left blank, for example? The test data that you choose will need to be listed and included in your project.

- Enter the first record, using the Tab key to move from field to field. You don't have to fill in every field – in fact as mentioned above you should test out the consequences of leaving some of them blank.

- Click **Add New** to save the first record and move to the second record.

- Once you've added about 6 records, click **OK** in the data form and you'll be returned to the main document.

Note: If you click **View Source** in the Data Form window, you will see all your data in tabular form as in Figure 16.5. To return to the main document, select **Tools**, **Mail Merge** again. Then select **Main Document**, **Edit** from the Mail Merge Helper.

Title	FirstName	LastName	JobTitle	Company	Address1	Address2	Town	County	PostalCode	HomePhone
Miss	Jane	Shepherd			65 Ferdinand Avenue		Colchester	Essex	CO5 4ER	01267 567890
Mr	Bernard	Newcastle	Managing Director	Pearl Fishers Inc	53-57 Cliff Court	Felixstowe		Suffolk	IP7 5HB	

Figure 16.5: The data source in Table view

Creating the form letter

The next stage is to write the letter that is to be sent out to customers, inserting merge fields wherever appropriate.

- You should have a blank document displayed on screen with the Mail Merge toolbar displayed above it. When you click the **Insert Merge Field** button on the Mail Merge toolbar, a list of your field names appears as shown below.

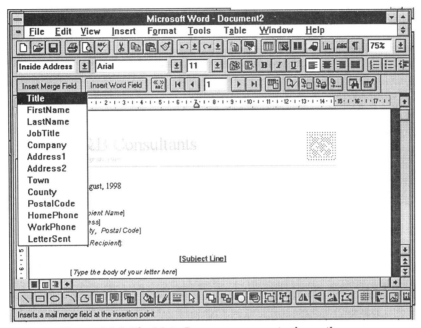

Figure 16.6: The Main Document screen in the mail merge

- To insert a merge field, click in the document where you want the first field inserted, then click **Insert Merge Field** and select the field from the drop-down list.

- Insert spaces, or press Enter whenever necessary. Your finished letter should look something like the one below.

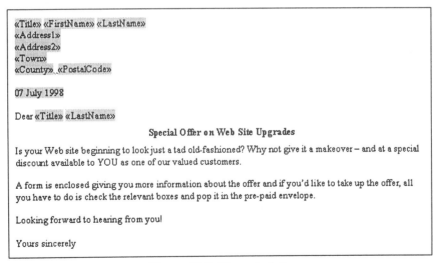

Figure 16.7: The main letter

- To view the letter with data in it, click the **View Merged Data** button on the Mail Merge toolbar to preview the merged document. The merge fields are replaced by the first record in the data source, as shown below.

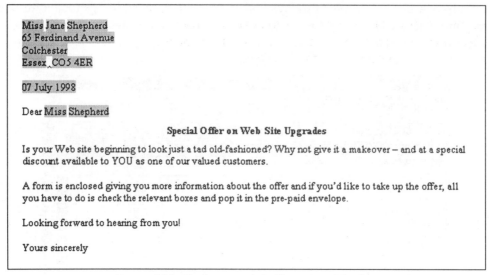

Figure 16.8: The letter with fields replaced by data

Note that letters should NOT begin 'Dear Miss Jane Shepherd' or 'Dear Jane Shepherd'. Either 'Dear Miss Shepherd' or more informally, 'Dear Jane' is acceptable. You will lose marks in your project for a letter containing errors in format, spelling and punctuation, so take care over it.

- The **View Merged Data** button is a toggle, so press it again to return to the main document.

- Save the document as *ABMerge.doc*.

Merging the data with the letter

- Select **Tools**, **Mail Merge** again.

- Click **Merge** and the following window appears:

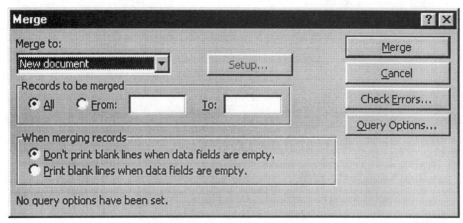

Figure 16.9: Merging the data

- The default is set to merge all records. The user could choose here to merge, for example, just records 5-6. For now, just click **Merge** to merge all the data.

- The letters with the names and addresses are shown on screen. You can now view them and print one or more letters.

- Notice that the letters themselves are given a default document name such as *Form Letters1*. You can save this document but you probably don't need to – the mail merge can be carried out again any time it is required. Close this document without saving.

Setting merge conditions

Frequently you don't want to send letters to everyone in the data set – you may want to mail only customers in Ipswich, customers whose invoices are overdue, or customers who have not already been mailed.

For example, suppose you have performed the mail merge as above, and over the next week or two you add some more potential customers to your mailing list to whom you want to send the same letter.

Or, supposing that once a week you look through your unpaid invoices and send a reminder to all customers who were invoiced over a month ago and still haven't paid. You don't want to repeatedly send the same reminder to the same customers week after week – so you need to be able to identify people who have already been mailed and exclude them from this week's mailing list. They can be removed from the list once they have paid up, or be identified as having paid, for example by setting a field called *Paid* in their record to 'Yes', or to the date when they paid.

Task 16.2: Send letters only to selected customers

In this task you will

- Set a 'flag' in each of the existing customers' records to indicate that they have been sent a letter;
- Add some new customers to the file;
- Set query options in the MailMerge Helper;
- Send letters only to customers who have not previously been mailed.

Setting a 'flag'

A *flag* is simply a field that you put a value in to indicate some condition or event. Earlier on we included a field called *LetterSent* in the record for each customer. Once the letter has been sent, we can set this to a suitable value – **y** for yes will do.

- Make sure the main document *ABMerge.doc* is open.

- Choose **Tools, Mail Merge** from the menu and under **Data Source**, select **Edit**. A popup list should appear listing your data source *Customer.doc*, as shown below.

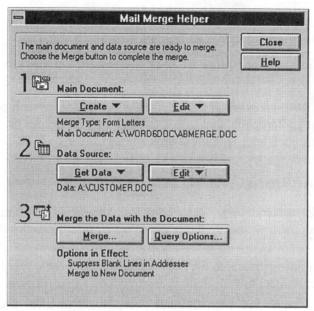

Figure 16.10: Editing the data source

- Click the data source (*C:\...\Customer.doc* or something similar) and the first record appears.

- Scroll down and click in the *LetterSent* field and type **y**.

- Click the **Next record** button at the bottom of the window and edit each record in turn.

- Click **OK** to return to the main document.

Setting the query options

- With the main document on screen select **Tools, Mail Merge** again and select **Query Options**.

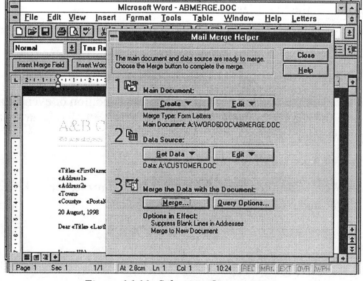

Figure 16.11: Selecting Query options

- The Query Options dialogue box is displayed. Select the **LetterSent** field from the drop-down list, **Not Equal To** for the Comparison, and type **y** in the third box as shown below. Click **OK**.

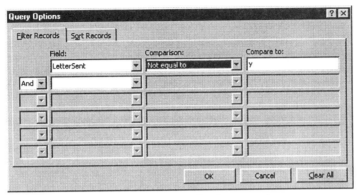

Figure 16.12: Setting the Query options

- Select **Merge** in the Mail Merge Helper window. Leave the defaults in the next window, and click **Merge**.

- You'll probably get an error message because none of your records fulfil the criteria you have set.

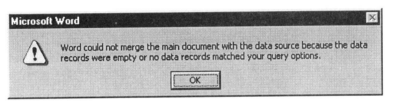

Figure 16.13

- Add a few new records, reset the query and try the merge again. You should find that only the new records have been merged.

Task 16.3: Send out club subscription reminders

In this task you will use conditional fields to vary the text of the letter sent out to different categories of club member. Senior members will be asked to pay an annual subscription of £20, and Junior members £10.

- Follow steps as in Task 1 to create a data source. You need to have a field called *MemberType*, and you can delete or edit other field names as you think appropriate.

- Enter some test data, making sure you have at least one Junior and one Senior member.

- Create the form letter, inserting merge fields for the name and address as in Task 1. The text of the letter is shown below.

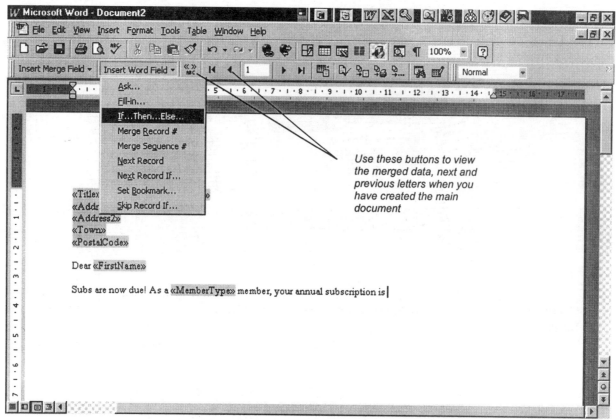

Figure 16.14: Creating a letter with an If..Then..Else field

- To insert the conditional field, click the **Insert Word Field** button as shown in the screen shot above. Select the **If..Then..Else** field.

- In the window fill in the field name, comparison and alternative text strings. Different letters will then have different text at this point.

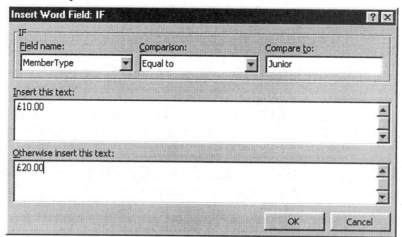

Figure 16.15: Inserting a conditional field

- You can browse through the letters as they will appear using the **View Merged Data**, **Next** and **Previous** buttons on the toolbar (see Figure 16.14.)

Displaying and editing field codes

You can display the field codes by highlighting (selecting) the field and pressing Shift-F9.

«Title» «FirstName» «LastName» «Address1»
«Address2»
«Town»
«PostalCode»

Dear «FirstName»

Subs are now due! As a «MemberType» member, your annual subscription is {IF {MERGEFIELD MemberType } = "Junior" "£10.00" "£20.00" }.

Etc etc.

Figure 16.16: Displaying field codes

You can edit the field directly when the field code is displayed. Try changing the subs to *£15* and *£30*.

Prompts to enter text

The **Fill-in** field will hold up the mail merge while you enter a specific value for each letter, or just for the first. You could, for example, have a Fill-in field for the date of the AGM.

- Add text to the letter: "The AGM this year will be held at 7.30pm on "

- Click on **Insert Word Field** and select **Fill-in**. A dialogue box appears.

- Enter a prompt "Enter the date of the AGM" and default Fill-in text: Thursday 20 May.

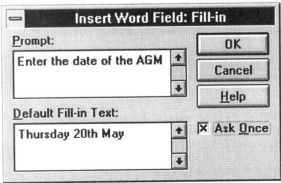

Figure 16.17: Fill-in field

- You'll be asked to enter the text again in the next dialogue box. Click **OK**.

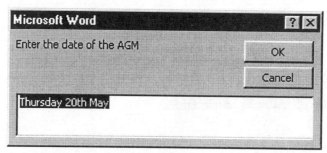

Figure 16.18: Entering the text for the Fill-in field

- Now try running the merge. You'll be prompted to enter the date of the AGM. If you checked the Ask Once box (see Figure 16.17) you won't be asked to enter the date for each individual letter.

- Close the letters document without saving, leaving the master document on screen.

Prompting for a different value for each member

Now suppose that you want to call each club member in for an audition (it's a drama club) and you want to specify a different audition time in each letter. The prompt needs to include the surname: for example, *Please enter audition time for Shepherd.*

- Add text to your letter: *Please come for an audition on 19ᵗʰ May at.*

- Click on **Insert Word Field** and select **Fill-in**. In the dialogue box, enter a prompt *Please enter audition time for* and default Fill-in text: *6pm*. This time, don't check the Ask Once box. As before, you'll be asked to enter the text again. Click **OK**.

- In the letter, press Shift-F9 to display the field code for the fill-in merge field.

        {FILLIN "Please enter audition time for " \d "6pm"}

- With the cursor positioned after the words *Please enter audition time for* click on **Insert Merge Field** and insert the *LastName* field. The field code will then appear as

        {FILLIN "Please enter audition time for {MERGEFIELD LastName}\d "6pm"}

- Now try running the merge. You'll be prompted to enter a time for each person in turn, for example "Please enter audition time for Shepherd".

Editing the data source

If you find that you need to add new fields to the Data Source, you can do this easily.

- Select **Tools, Mail Merge** from the Main document.

- Select **Data Source, Edit** in the Mail Merge Helper.

- Select **View Data Source** from the Data Form window. (See Figure 16.4)

- Add or delete columns as required while in Table view.

- Save the document and select **Tools, Mail Merge** again. **Main Document, Edit** returns you to the Main document.

Internal and external data sources

In this chapter we have used an **internal data source** – in other words, the details of customers or club members were created in Word and stored as a Word document. Word also allows you to use an **external data source** – such as a table created in MS Access, for example. You simply specify the file you need as the Data source in the Mail Merge Helper dialogue box.

This feature is very useful if the user already has a database of customers and wants to be able to send letters to all or some of them. Although your project should not use more than one software package, it is perfectly acceptable to import an external data source.

Additional tasks

Look at other options in the Mail Merge. You can, for example, merge the data from just one or two specified records. (Look again at Figure 16.9.) Or, you can use a query to specify for example the surname of a single individual to whom you wish to send a letter. Alternatively, the Mail Merge toolbar has buttons to enable a user to quickly find the record containing a particular first name or surname, for example.

Find record

Figure 16.19: The Mail Merge toolbar

Pressing the **Find Record** button brings up a dialogue box:

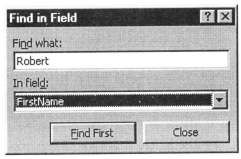

Figure 16.20: Finding a particular record

The record number indicator will then display the appropriate record number so that the user can then elect to send the letter to just that person.

If you don't think the Mail Merge toolbar is particularly user-friendly, in the next chapter you'll learn how to create your own toolbar buttons.

Consider whether these options would be useful to the user for whom you are developing your project.

Chapter 17 – Customising Menus and Toolbars

Introduction

In Chapter 14 we had a brief look at how to put a new button on a toolbar. In this chapter we'll put a new menu item on the menu bar. **Word 7 users should follow the instructions in this chapter.**

Suppose that your user has three or four people that he or she regularly writes to – people like the company accountant, a major supplier, a co-author or partner. It's a nuisance to have to type in their name and address every time a letter has to be written. We'll automate the process so that all the user has to do is select a **Letters** option from the menu, and then pick the recipient from a drop-down list to open a new document with the name and address already entered.

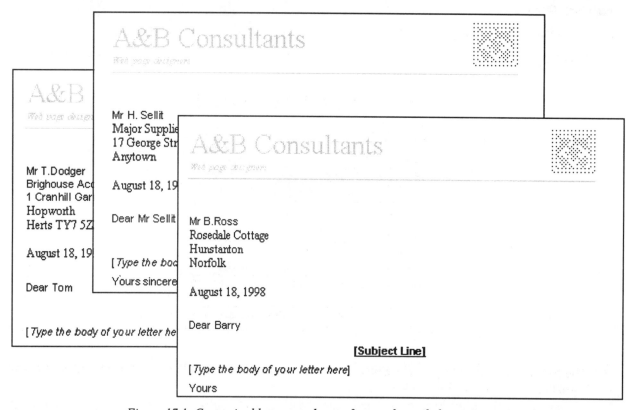

Figure 17.1: Customised letter template to frequently-mailed recipients

Task 17.1: Create a custom menu to open various letter templates

In this task you will first record macros to insert suitable text (e.g. names and addresses) in each of several letters, and then create a menu of options to run these macros.

Creating the customised templates

We need to record macros to open each of the blank letters and insert the appropriate text.. Each macro will

- Open a new document based on the *ABLetter.dot* template. (If you are working on a network, it will be simplest to try out the task in this chapter using the standard template *Normal.dot*. In your project, it would make sense to open a new document based on the specially created template that has the company letterhead already present.)

- Enter the recipient's name and address, greeting and closing lines.

You have to consider where you are going to save the macro. Any macros that you save in *Normal.dot* will be available in all documents, but you won't be able to save anything in *Normal.dot* on a College network. We will save the macros in the template *ABNormal* which was created in Chapter 12.

● Open *MainDoc*, the document based on *ABNormal.dot*.

● Select **Tools**, **Macro**.

● Click **Record**.

● Select **Documents Based On ABNormal.dot** in the Make Macro Available To box.

● Name the macro *Accountant* and type a description. Click **OK**.

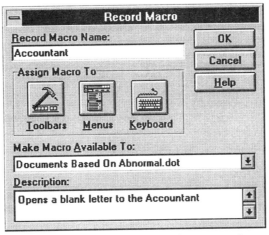

Figure 17.2: Choosing the location for storing the macro

● The macro starts recording. Click **File**, **New** to open a new document based either on *ABLetter.dot* or *Normal.dot*.

● Type in the first recipient's name and address, greeting and closing line. This letter will be to the accountant. Note that you must use the keyboard arrow keys and not the mouse when recording a macro; clicking the mouse somewhere in the document cannot be recorded because the macro does not know where you are clicking relative to the current document. You can use Shift and the arrow keys to move in and out of fields.

● Leave the cursor positioned where the user will normally start typing.

● Stop the macro.

● Close the new document without saving.

- Repeat the above steps twice more, creating macros called *Supplier* and *Partner*.

Adding a custom menu

- Have the document *MainDoc* open on screen.

- Select **Tools**, **Customize** and then click the **Menus** tab.

- In the Save Changes In box, select **ABNormal.dot**.

- Click **Menu Bar** (the bottom button on the right hand side).

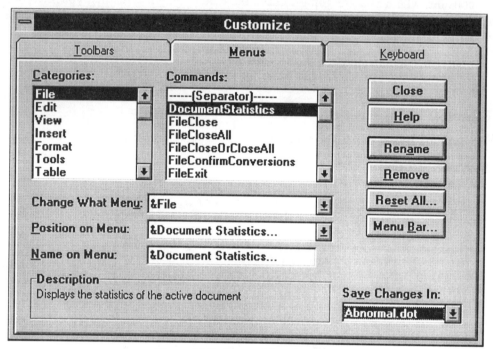

Figure 17.3: Customising the menu

- In the next window, enter the name *&Letters*. (The & before L makes Alt-L the shortcut key. You will see that the L appears underlined in the menu.)

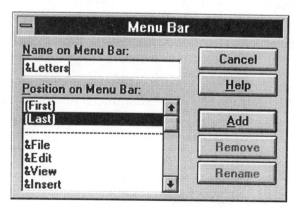

Figure 17.4: Naming the menu

- Click **Add** and then click **Close**. Click **Close** in the other window. Your new menu appears, but it doesn't do anything yet.

- To add a command to the custom menu, click **Tools**, **Customize**. Make sure the **Menus** tab is selected.

- Click **Macros** in the Categories box. Select *ABNormal.dot* in the Save Changes In box. Select **&Letters** in the Change What Menu box, select the *Accountant* macro, and select **At Bottom** in Position on Menu. (See Figure 17.5.)

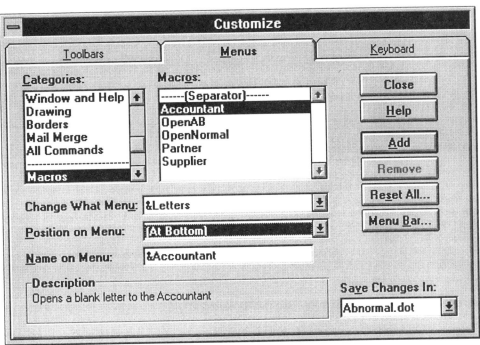

Figure 17.5: Adding a command to the menu

- Click **Add**.

- Now select *Partner* and click **Add**. Then add *Supplier* in the same way.

- Click **Close**.

- Try out the new menu.

- Save *MainDoc.doc*.

- Close *MainDoc.doc*. Click **Yes** when asked if you want to save changes to *ABNormal.dot*.

Creating a toolbar

Instead of, or as well as, adding a new menu to the menu bar, you can create your own customised toolbar. The toolbar buttons can have either text or graphics on them, and can be used to run any of the macros that you have created.

Task 17.2: Create a custom toolbar

In this task you will create a brand new toolbar named A&B Toolbar which will have buttons to run the three macros *Accountant*, *Partner* and *Supplier*.

- From the **View** menu, select **Toolbars**.

- Click the **New** button.

- In the Toolbar name box, type the name *A&B Toolbar*.

- In the Make Toolbar Available To box, select *ABNormal.dot*. Click **OK**.

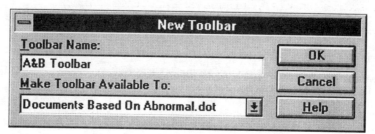

Figure 17.6: Creating a new toolbar

- The toolbar appears on the screen as a small square. In the Customize dialogue box, select *ABNormal* in the Save Changes In box. In the Categories box, select **Macros**.

- Drag the macro *Accountant* to the toolbar and click **Assign**.

- Repeat for *Partner* and *Supplier*.

This completes the task. You can now test out the toolbar buttons.

Chapter 18 – Adding a Front End

Creating an application

So far you've created several types of documents and templates that would be useful to a user. Now it's time to review exactly what the user needs in the way of templates, mail-merge options and so on, and provide an easy way for each of these options to be accessed.

You could, for example:

- Create a customised toolbar with options for the user to choose from;

- Add a customised menu to the menu bar;

- Use a combination of both the above.

When you work on your project, you will have to decide how the user will start up his customised system. One option might be that as soon as Word is loaded, the document *MainDoc* automatically appears and displays the company name and logo along with some sort of Welcome message. The custom toolbar and menu would also appear.

Creating macros that run automatically

You can create five macros that will run under certain conditions:

6   Any macro that you name *AutoExec* runs when you start Word.

7   Any macro that you name *AutoNew* runs when you create a new document.

8   Any macro that you name *AutoOpen* runs when you open a new document.

9   Any macro that you name *AutoClose* runs when you close a document. .

10   Any macro that you name *AutoExit* runs when you exit Word. .

AutoExec and *AutoExit* have to be stored in *Normal.dot*, and the others can be stored in any template. If you are working on a network, you will not be able to store the *AutoExec* macro in *Normal.dot*. Probably the best alternative for the purposes of demonstrating your project, is for the user to manually open *MainDoc* when starting a session. This will ensure that the customised template with all its macros, menus and toolbars is loaded.

If you install the system for a real user on a computer with no access restrictions, you can create an Autoexec macro, saved in *Normal.dot* which opens *MainDoc*.

Part 4

Tackling the Project

In this section:

Chapter 19 – Starting Your Project

Selecting a suitable project

The first hurdle to overcome is to find a suitable application to develop. You need to find a user, typically the owner of a small business, a Club secretary, or someone who uses a word processor in their office environment and performs specific tasks on a regular basis. The more you understand about exactly what the user does and what would make their tasks easier, the better your project will be. Therefore, try to get involved and spend some time with the user watching and helping, if possible.

Possible scenarios

A typical word processing project may be based around one of the following two ideas. If you choose one of these ideas on which to base your project, you should adapt it for a real club or business and customise it to a real user's requirements. An I.T. project is not simply about using a computer to do clever things – it is about understanding a real user's problems and using I.T. to help them run an organisation more efficiently. At the same time, you should seek out opportunities to demonstrate the advanced features of Word, rather than, for example, spending a long time designing a logo, which will gain very few marks. Be selective and aim for depth rather than breadth in your choice of tasks – the more automated and customised the solution, the higher the grade you are likely to get.

1. **Sports Club/Drama Club etc.**

   You are asked to design and implement a customised word processing system for a Club to perform the following tasks (not necessarily all of them!):

   - Create printed stationery incorporating Club name, address and logo, and the Secretary's name and telephone number.

   - Create templates for letters, invoices, memos, minutes of meetings.

   - Keep a list of members' names, and details such as address, date of birth, availability, etc.

   - Send out standard letters to all or selected members to advise them of subscriptions due, match fixtures, etc.

   - Send out invoices and reminders to members who have not paid subscriptions.

2. **Small Business Word Processing System**

   You are asked to create a customised system for a small business to automate some of the tasks which are performed regularly. The system could typically enable a user to:

   - Create printed stationery incorporating Business name and address, logo, telephone, fax and e-mail numbers, VAT registration number if appropriate, Directors' or Proprietors' names.

   - Create templates for some of the following: letters, fax header sheets, memos, With Compliments slips, invoices, orders, remittance slips and business cards.

   - Enter details of customers, including possibly their requirements or their payment status.

   - Send standard letters to all or selected customers informing them of new products, events or special offers, or reminders if invoices have not been paid, and print envelopes.

The mark scheme

Turn to the Appendix at the end of this book, which contains the NEAB instructions and guidance for project work. You will see that the mark scheme in Section 7.22 is divided into three sections: **Analysis and Design, Implementation and Testing**, and **Evaluation**. You could organise your project report into these three major sections, but you may choose to vary this. Analysis and Design, for example, are really two independent sections. Also, looking in more detail at the mark scheme under Implementation and Testing, you will see that marks are given for providing effective test data and evidence of testing, and for 'detailed user and technical documentation'. This section could well be broken down into Implementation and Testing, Technical Documentation and User Manual. The third section of the mark scheme, Evaluation, can stay as one section.

Spend some time familiarising yourself with the mark scheme so you know exactly what you are aiming for. Ultimately the decision on how best to structure the report is yours.

Creating an outline for your project

Word has a useful feature called **Outlining**. This feature enables you to create an outline for your entire project, breaking it down into sections and sub-sections, which you can then fill in as you build up your project. You can easily add, delete or rearrange headings at any stage, and at the end of it all you will be able to create an automatic Table of Contents.

Task 19.1: Create an outline for your project

In this task you will use Word's Outline feature to create an outline for your project. You can do this even before you have selected your project. It will help you to get a clear idea of the kind of task you should be setting yourself.

- Open a new document using the *Normal* template and save it as *Project.doc*.

- Click the **Outline View** button at the lower left corner of the Word window.

Figure 19.1: The Outline View button

- The Outline toolbar pops up, the Style box displays Heading 1 style, and a fat minus sign appears in the left margin.

Figure 19.2: The Outline toolbar

- Type your first heading *Analysis* and press Enter.

- Now type the first subtopic heading, *Introduction*. It also gets Heading 1 style, just like the first heading. Since you want it to be a subtopic, click it and then click the **Demote** tool on the Outline toolbar. That makes it a Heading 2 style.

- Type the other headings for the Analysis section. These could include:

> *Objectives*
> *Hardware and Software*
> *User's Skill Level*

- Press Enter after *User's Skill Level*, click the **Promote** tool and type the next major heading: ***Design***.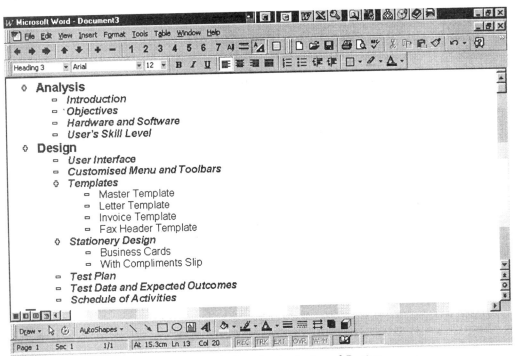

- The headings in the Design section will obviously depend on what you are designing. Typically, the Design may break down into the following:

> *User Interface*
> *Customised Menu and Toolbars*
> *Templates*
> > *Master Template*
> > *Letter Template*
> > *Invoice Template*
> > *Fax Header Template*
> *Stationery Design*
> > *Business Cards*
> > *With Compliments Slip*
> *Test Plan*
> *Test data and Expected Outcomes*
> *Schedule of Activities*

- Add these headings and subheadings to your outline. At this stage your screen should look something like Figure 19.3.

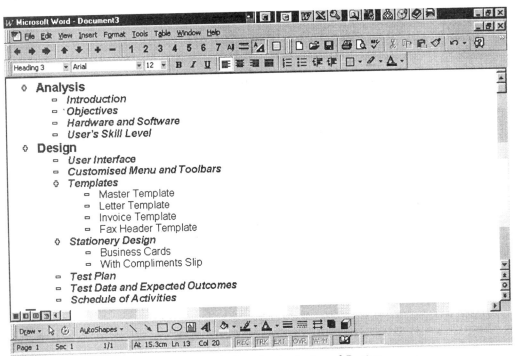

Figure 19.3: Outline for Analysis and Design

- Now enter the headings for the next four major headings: *Implementation and Testing, Technical Documentation, User Manual* and *Evaluation*. These are all at Heading 1 level.

This completes the project outline. Naturally, you will probably want to amend it as you develop your own ideas.

Reordering topics

If you decide that you want to change the order of topics in your project, do the following:

- Select for example *Schedule of Activities*. To move it up to the top of the Design section, click the Move Up button several times until it reaches the top of the section.

Adding numbers to the headings

- Select **Format, Bullets and Numbering**.

- Click the **Outline Numbered** tab and select a numbering format or customise one to your own liking. Your outline will appear something like Figure 19.4.

Note: If you decide to move your outline headings up or down it's a good idea to remove the numbers first and then re-apply them.

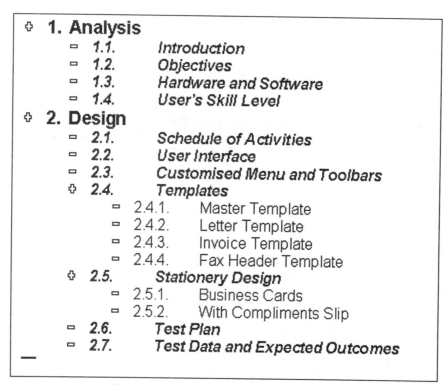

Figure 19.4: Adding numbers to an outline

Turning the outline into a document

The outline IS the document. Just click the **Normal View** button at the bottom of the window, and start entering text. You may want to change the indent and make a new style for the document text.

Adding a header and footer

You should add a header and footer to your project documentation. For example, the header could contain the Project title and the Section title, and the footer could contain your name and the page number.

● Insert page breaks between each of your major sections by pressing Ctrl-Enter wherever you want a page break.

● With the cursor at the beginning of the project outline, select **View, Header and Footer**.

● On the left hand side of the header, type your project title.

● Tab twice to get to the right hand side of the header. We need to insert a field here so that the name of the section is inserted.

● Select **Insert, Field**. In the **Categories** box select **Links and References**. In the Field Names box, select StyleRef.

● After the word STYLEREF, enter the style name "Heading 1" in quotes as shown in Figure 19.5.

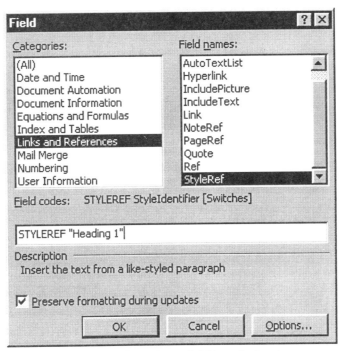

Figure 19.5: Inserting a field into the header

● Click OK. The header should appear as in Figure 19.6.

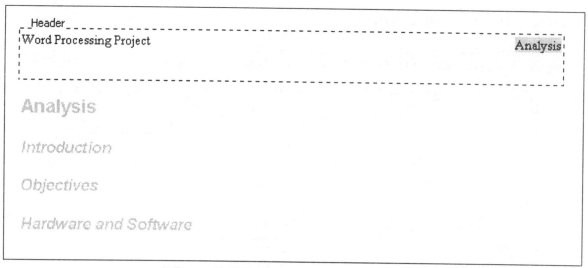

Figure 19.6: Header containing Section name

- Click the **Switch between Header and Footer** button and insert your name and the page number.

Inserting a Table of Contents

You can now insert a Table of Contents at the beginning of your project. This can be automatically updated at any time by clicking in it and pressing F9.

- Insert a page break in front of the heading *Analysis*.

- Click the **Normal View** button in the bottom left of the Word window (or select **View, Normal**).

- With the cursor at the beginning of the document, click **Insert, Index and Tables**.

- Click the **Table of Contents** tab. Leave the other defaults as shown in Figure 19.7.

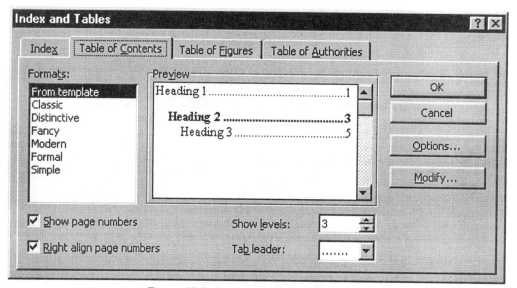

Figure 19.7: Inserting a Table of Contents

● The table of contents will appear as shown below.

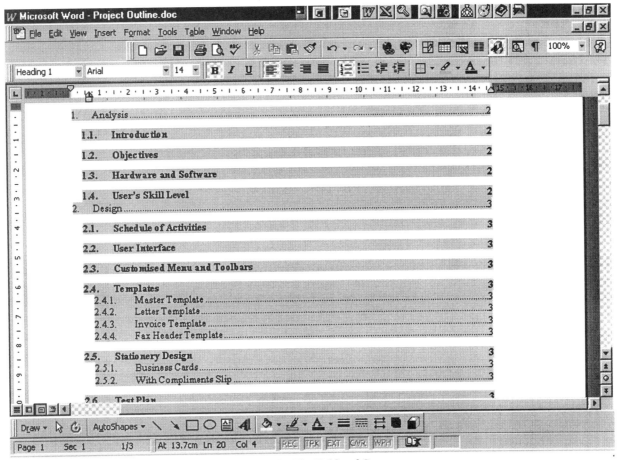

Figure 19.8: The Table of Contents

● You can change the styles of TOC1, TOC2 etc which are used in the Table of Contents using **Format, Style**.

● You can also change the styles of Heading 1, Heading 2 etc.

That's about it for your project outline. In the next few chapters we'll flesh out each section.

Chapter 20 – Analysis and Design

A top-down approach

Adopting a top-down approach to your project means that you first identify the main tasks which have to be performed. Then you break each of these tasks into increasing level of detail. In the last chapter you saw how to create an outline for the project documentation, and that gives you a good general idea of the major tasks to be performed, which are to:

- Choose a project and interview the user to establish the objectives, hardware and software to be used, user's skill level;

- Design the various parts of the system, writing it up as you go;

- Implement the system;

- Test the system;

- Evaluate the system;

- Write the User and Technical manuals;

- Put the finishing touches to your project documentation.

Next, break down each of these tasks where possible. Analysis, for example, will involve both establishing what is required and documenting your findings. Design will involve designing the individual templates, macros etc, consultation with the user and writing up the design. Implementation will involve working on the computer to turn your design into a working system. Testing will involve making sure that everything works as planned, with correct results being obtained whatever data, valid or invalid, is entered. Evaluation means looking back at the original objectives and making an honest appraisal of how well these have been fulfilled. Completing the user manual may involve running the system and taking screen shots, which can be very time-consuming.

Performing the analysis

The analysis involves finding out exactly what the user's requirements are. You need to have worked through most of the first section of this book before doing the analysis so that you know what is possible within Word. Then you need to interview the user. Your documentation should include a brief description of the organisation you are developing the project for, and a list of objectives. A sample Analysis section is given below. Do **NOT** copy this slavishly – figure out your own user's objectives and write them up in your own words!

Do be aware that moderators and teachers are familiar with textbooks such as this one and are always on the lookout for work that has simply been copied. You MUST produce original work, so use the textbook to learn new techniques and to get ideas, and then apply them to your own chosen project. You will not score highly for a project that simply changes the title of the company to C&D Consultants and produces identical objectives, stationery, invoices and business cards – and believe me, some students don't even go to the trouble of changing the name of the company!

Analysis

Introduction

James Brady is setting up a small business partnership to design Web sites for small businesses and educational establishments. He and a friend Jo Anderson have already successfully installed several Web sites and their reputation is growing in the area.

James runs the business side of things and plans eventually to use an Accounts package to keep track of the financial side of the business. However in the meantime, with only a few customers, he is writing invoices by hand and keeping accounts using a spreadsheet package, but he would like to send out more professional-looking invoices. In addition, he intends to use MS Word to deal with day-to-day correspondence and for sending out reminders to customers who have not paid their invoices.

Objectives *(this could include "performance indicators")*

The objectives of the project are listed below:

1. Design stationery for the business. This must include

    Letter stationery

    With Compliments slip

    Fax header sheet

    Business cards

The stationery must look attractive and professional, and must contain all the required information such as business name, address, telephone number etc.

2. Create templates for the various different types of stationery, automating text entry wherever possible, for example eliminating the need to type 'Yours sincerely', 'Yours faithfully', 'Best wishes' etc every time.

3. In the letter template, include a quick and easy way for James to enter the name and address of people he frequently has to write to, e.g. his accountant, his partner Jo Anderson and an Internet service provider that he regularly uses.

4. To automate as far as possible the production of invoices.

5. To enable James to identify late payers and send them a first and if necessary, second letter requesting payment.

6. To be able to identify which customers have been sent a reminder, and to be able to easily amend records of customers who have paid and therefore do not need further reminders.

7. To be able to keep records of all customers and send them letters advertising other services.

8. To be able to print off business cards, fax header sheets, With Compliments slips and blank headed stationery whenever required.

Performance indicators

(Relate your performance indicators to the objectives in such a way that when you come to do the evaluation, you can look back at this section and compare what you set out to achieve with the end result. Some of these may be qualitative "All the business documents have a consistent and pleasing appearance". Others may be quantitative: "An invoice can be prepared in n minutes.")

Hardware and Software

James has the following hardware and software available:

- A Pentium 266MHz PC with 32Mb RAM, 4Gb hard drive, floppy disk drive, CD ROM drive.

(You could also discuss here the capabilities or limitations of the hardware in relation to the requirements of the project.)

- Laser printer.

- Windows 97.

- Office 97.

The system will however be developed and tested on a College network using Office 97, which poses various problems. These are discussed in the Design Section.

User's skill level

James is expert in the use of a PC and uses Word 97 regularly but does not make any use of advanced features such as customised toolbars, templates, macros and fields. He would like the customised system to be as straightforward and obvious as possible, not involving memorising various different key combinations to achieve the desired result.

Planning a schedule of activities

Once you have chosen the project and established the objectives you should have a fair idea of the amount of work involved. You will probably have been given a deadline for handing in your project, so you know how much time is available. Drawing up a schedule is not only a required part of your project, it is an essential part of Project Management, whether the project is designing a software system or building the Channel Tunnel. You must know at all times if you are up to schedule or falling behind.

Your schedule should show what you plan to do in each week until you finish the project. Each week should include some tasks that can be done at home and some that can be done in school or College.

A sample schedule of activities is shown below. Use it as a guide but remember it is extremely unlikely to be suitable for your particular project so you must write your own.

Schedule of Activities

Week	Task	Home/School	Comment
1	Find out exactly what information needs to go on the stationery.	H	
1	Create several designs for letterheads and show to user to comment and/or select one.	H/S	
1	Design user interface.	H	
2	Create template for letter to incorporate letter head, macro for allowing user to enter addressee etc.	S	
2	Write up Analysis.	H/S	
3	Create Invoice template.	S	
3	Create With Comps slip, Fax header, business cards.	H/S	
4	Agree text of letters for first and second reminders for late payees.	H	
4	Create mail merge letters and database in Word of names and addresses	S	

4	Create queries to pick out only people who have not already been sent 1st/2nd reminder, whose payment is overdue.	S	
5	Create test plan and test data to test all templates and mail merge	H/S	
5	Write up Design	H/S	
6	Implement user interface with front end menu.	S	
6	Carry out testing and produce screen shots showing test output.	S	
7	Write the user manual, which will include a description of the manual procedures which need to be followed.	H/S	
8	Write up technical manual	H/S	
8	Demonstrate the completed system to the user and get user feedback. Incorporate any suggested improvements where possible. Ask user for written feedback.	H	
9	Write up evaluation and complete the project report. Hand it in.	H/S	

Tackling the design

The Design is probably the hardest part of the whole project. You have to show in detail how you are going to implement each part of the project. This will involve, for example:

- Designing a schedule of activities. You must plan how you are going to complete your project in the time allowed.

- Deciding what the user interface should look like – will there be a menu screen for the user to select from? Will there be custom menu bars and toolbars?

- Producing hand-drawn designs of templates showing what will go on each;

- Showing the designs to the user, to ensure that they are exactly what is required;

- Designing any macros which are needed to automate tasks;

- Designing a comprehensive test plan and test data, and working out what the expected outcome of each test is. This is a lengthy and painstaking business!

You have to write up the design in such a way that it could be implemented by a competent person – in other words, someone possessing at least the same level of skills as yourself.

Designing the user interface

Depending on which version of Word you are using, you may or may not be able to put command buttons on a full-screen menu. However you will be able to make a custom menu on the menu bar and a customised toolbar. You may decide to use a combination of several different methods – Word often has half a dozen ways of performing a task like cutting and pasting or saving a document.

Use a pencil and paper to work out what menus and toolbars you are going to use and include your hand-drawn design, as in Figure 20.1. You may wish the end-user to sign off your designs as proof that you have discussed them in detail.

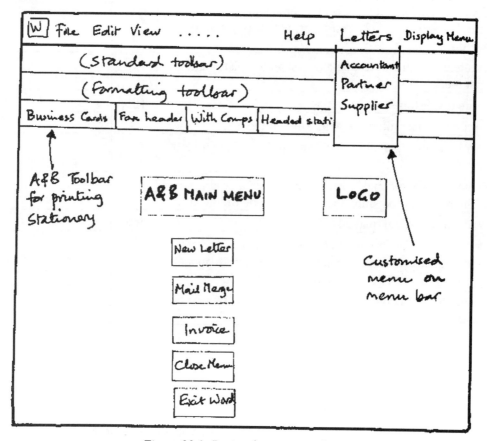

Figure 20.1: Design for user interface

Make sure you have included an easy way for the user to perform all the tasks stated in the objectives. You may need more than one level of menu: for example, once the letter template is loaded, a customised tool for printing envelopes should appear. Similarly, in the invoice window there may be a customised button to update fields, and there may be special buttons in the Mail Merge window. Think about what is required and explain graphically or otherwise what custom buttons you will be implementing.

Macros

In the Design section you can describe the function of the macros that you intend to use, such as macros which are run when buttons on the custom toolbar are pressed. In the Technical Documentation you can show the Visual Basic code that was created automatically, and any code you have added yourself. Indicate where each macro is to be stored, for example in a particular document or template. *Remember to distinguish between code automatically generated, e.g. by a recorder, and original code written by you.*

Design of stationery

All the stationery used by the business will have the company name, address, telephone number, fax number, and logo on it. If the company has a turnover of less than £50,000 p.a. it will probably not be VAT registered so will not need a VAT registration number to be shown. If the business is a sole trader or partnership rather than a limited company, the names of the owner(s) will be shown as the proprietors (rather than Directors). If it is a club the secretary's name will probably appear somewhere.

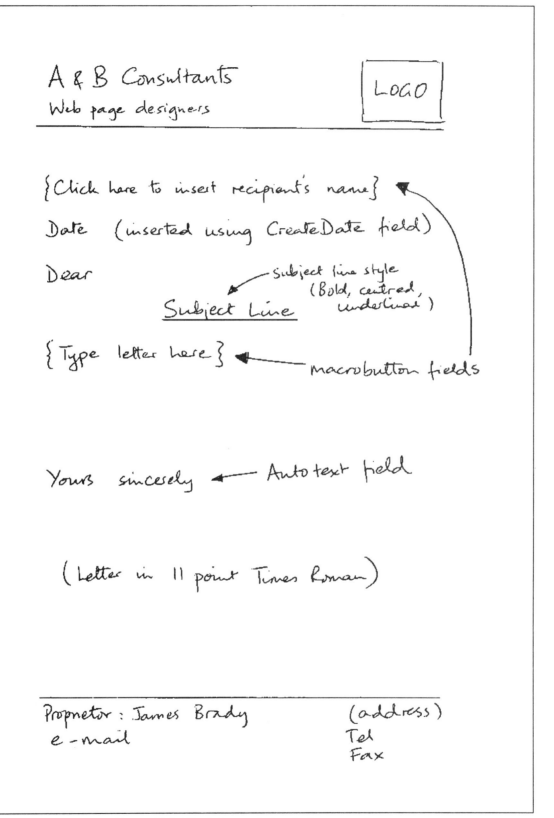

Figure 20.2: Hand-drawn design for letter template

You should plan out using paper and pencil what each of your business stationery templates will look like. Indicate styles, autotext entries, fields, macrobutton fields and so on. Remember that using these designs *someone else* should be able to implement your system.

Master template

For reasons that were explained in Parts 2 and 3 of this book, it is rather important to base all your templates around a single master template, whether this is the *Normal* template or a customised template. This will ensure that any macros, custom menus and toolbars stored in this template are available in all documents based on the master template. You should explain this in your design, specifying for each document which template it is based on. For example:

Templates

Since the development work is to be done on a school network it will not be possible to store templates in the default templates directory or to store any macro, customised toolbars or menus in the *Normal* template. Therefore a master template named *ABNormal* will be created as follows:

- Load a new file as a template using the Normal template (Blank document).

- Save this template on A: naming it *ABNormal.dot*.

A custom menu, toolbar and full screen menu with command buttons will be placed in *ABNormal.dot*. Two master documents based on this template will be created. The master document *ABMaster* will be a blank document containing the company name, address, logo and other details. *Maindoc* will act as the user front end.

Both these documents will be created by opening a new blank document using the *Normal* template, and then attaching the template *ABNormal.dot*.

Letter template (*ABLetter.dot*, created by amending *ABMaster.dot*)

Three possible designs were shown to the user. *(Show these in an Appendix.)* The chosen design is shown in Figure 20.2.

The letter template will include the following:

- Header showing company logo and company name.

- Footer showing proprietor's name, address, telephone number, fax number and e-mail address. No VAT registration number is necessary for this particular business.

- A MACROBUTTON field which runs an empty macro named NoMacro. This enables 'placeholder text' to be placed in the document for the user to click on to insert addressee's name and address and subject of letter.

- Appropriate styles for the different types of text in the letter. E.g. the 'Subject' style will be bold, centred and underlined. Normal letter text will be 11pt Times Roman, left-justified. Footer text will be 8pt Times Roman.

- Field for today's date.

- Field for closing. The user will be able to select from options such as 'Yours faithfully', 'Yours sincerely' or 'Best wishes' or type an alternative.

Invoice template

(etc)

Note that business cards and With Compliment slips don't require a template from which the user loads a new document and enters text. They are simply documents which the user can print out when required, and amend if necessary. They can be made 'Read-only recommended' to prevent accidental alteration. A Fax header sheet may be used in one of two ways – the user can print out blank Fax header sheets so that hand-written faxes can be sent, or sometimes the user may want to type a Fax using the Fax Header template.

Try to get hold of a range of With Compliment slips and fax header sheets to give yourself some design ideas. Figure 20.3 shows different designs for business cards.

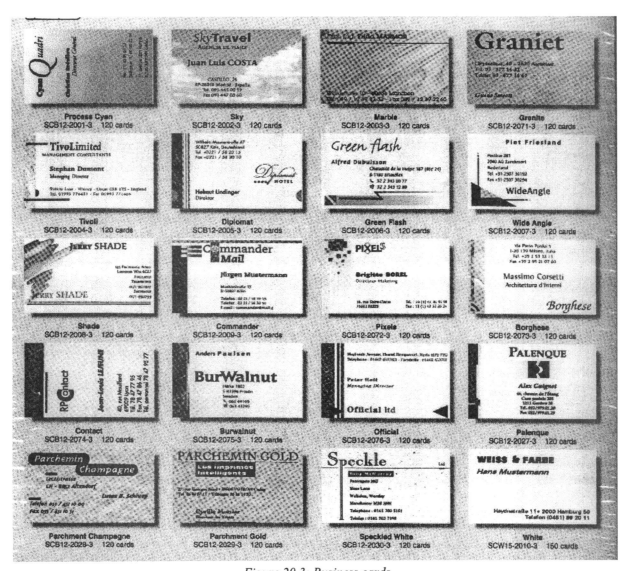

Figure 20.3: Business cards

Mail merge

If your project includes a mail merge you need to specify whether you are using an internal or external data source, and what the data fields are. You also need to show what fields are placed on the mail merge letter, and explain how the user is going to use the mail merge to send a letter to just one person or to a selected group, for example all customers who have unpaid invoices over 30 days old. This is where your problem-solving skills will be tested — you have to fully understand the problem you are trying to solve and come up with a solution. It is not enough simply to place fields on a letter and then merge it with every record in the data source.

Try to include some of the more advanced features like query options and fill-in fields. Make sure the text of your letter is correctly laid out (e.g. Dear Mr Mukit, NOT Dear Abdul Mukit), correctly spelt and grammatically flawless.

In your test output, there is no need to include as evidence **all** the printouts from a mailmerge. Show the test data and then selective printouts to prove that all aspects of the mail merge work.

Test plan

The test plan has several aspects to it. It should include:

- A test strategy;
- Test data;
- A list of tests to be performed with expected results.

The test strategy should be briefly described. For example:

Test Plan

Test strategy

A full range of tests will be carried out on the computer used for development work. This will include:

- Testing each item on the full-screen menu to ensure that each command button functions correctly;
- Testing each custom menu item on the menu bar;
- Testing each button on the custom toolbar to ensure that the correct document is opened;
- Testing each template by using it with test data;
- Testing all aspects of the mail merge with carefully selected test data to ensure that the query options and fields are all working correctly;
- Testing the invoice with carefully selected test data to ensure that every formula gives the expected result.

Once the system is working correctly it will be installed on the user's machine. This will involve making minor changes to change path names in several macros which refer to templates currently saved on the A: drive. The full range of tests will therefore be carried out again on the user's machine.

The user will then be asked to test the system to ensure that nothing has been forgotten or left out, and no requirements misinterpreted.

Test data

Invoice

The following test data will be used to test the invoice.

(Current date and time)	Invoice number 12345
Invoice address	Customer order number ABC/123
Mrs V Smith	Delivery address
123 Church Street	2 Riverside Ave
Woodbridge	Woodbridge
Suffolk	
IP12 2WE	

Qty	Product description	Price per item	Net Amount	VAT rate	VAT Amount
1	Item 1	10.00	*(10.00)*	17.5	*(1.75)*
10	Item 2	5	*(50.00)*	10.0	*(5.00)*
100	Item 3	0.06	*(6.00)*	17.5	*(6.30)*
20	Item 4	10.50	*(210.00)*	17.5	*(36.75)*
33	Refund	2.99	*(-98.67)*	15.00	*(-14.80)*
	CARRIAGE	5.50			
	TOTAL NET		*(177.33)*		
	TOTAL VAT		*(35.00)*		
	TOTAL INVOICE VALUE		*(217.83)*		

Notes:

This data tests every line of the invoice.

The expected results are given in italics in brackets.

The time is included with the date so that the invoice can be closed and reopened to check that the time still shows the time of creation of the invoice, not the current time. The time will be deleted from the template when this has been checked.

Mail Merge

The following test data will be used to test the mail merge.

Title	FirstName	LastName	Address 1	Address 2	Town	County	Post Code	HomePhone	WorkPhone	Letter Sent
Mr	George	Wilson	*(fill in)*							Y
Miss	Gerri	Adams								Y
Mr	Robert	Mills								N
Mrs	Kate	Watson								X
Mr	Ken	Bates								N

Show what records you will put in the data source. Then show the query options that will be used and the values of any Fill-in fields and state what you expect to happen.)

Show all the test data you will use, and be sure to include both valid and invalid data.

Tests

Test No	Test	Expected result	Comment /verified
1	Test 'Display menu' button on menu bar	Main menu should display	
2	Test 'Accountant' option on Letters menu	New letter should open with name and address of Accountant. Envelope button should appear on toolbar	
3	Test Business cards button and open for printing only	Password dialogue box should appear. On clicking Read Only button, Business cards should appear. These can be printed but not modified.	
4	Test Business cards button and open for modification.	Password dialogue box should appear. On entering the password 'modify', business cards should open and modifications can be made.	
5-10	*(Test all buttons and menu items)*		
11	Test Invoice with test data given above.	Expected values as calculated manually in test data should appear. Today's date and current time appear	
12	Close Invoice and reopen.	Time field should not change (so date won't change tomorrow either)	
13	Add the data given above to the Mail merge data source.	Data accepted.	
14	Perform mail merge with Merge Letter (Special Offer) to all customers	Letters to all customers created	
15	Update customer records so that LetterSent=Y	Records updated	
16	Insert 2 new customers Shepherd and Moss	Records added	
17	Set Query Options so that letter only goes to customers with LetterSent = N	Letters created only for Shepherd and Moss.	
18	Use FindRecord button to find record for Watson	Should be the 4th record.	
19	Perform Mail merge for record 4 only	Only one letter created.	
20	*Etc.*		

Chapter 21 – Implementation and Testing

How is the implementation assessed?

Marks are given for fully implementing the design unaided, and with no obvious defects. To get good marks the project must use advanced facilities of the software in an appropriate manner. Since the moderator will not actually see your project running, your teacher will test and mark the project and verify the degree to which it actually works, and the teacher's comments, together with your project report, are then sent to the moderator to ensure that a consistent standard is applied right across the country. You must provide written evidence that the project works, and this will largely be done by including test output in the form of screen shots and printed reports, documents or letters produced by your system. The User Manual and Technical Manual are also marked in this section and will provide more evidence of a working system.

In the Appendix you will find Instructions and Guidance on the Internal Assessment of Coursework. Read this carefully because it will help you to understand what marks are awarded for. For example, point 7.11.6 suggests that for a Major Project you should 'compile an ongoing record giving reasons for each decision made'. Even for a Minor Project this could be included in the Implementation and Testing Section, although it is not obligatory, as it will provide important evidence of your having actually carried out the work. **(Word is not a suitable choice of package for a Major Project.)** Have your project folder handy whenever you are working on your project and jot down handwritten notes which you can type up later. For example:

Ongoing record of implementation progress and problems

Week 1 -   I used a program called 'Paint Shop Pro' to design the company logo, and showed 3 different designs to the user who chose the second one. *(Then show the 3 versions.)*

...

Week 6 -   I was going to have the main menu come up automatically using an Autoexec macro but I cannot do this on the network. Therefore I have had to modify the design and put a 'Display Menu' button on the menu bar in a document called *Maindoc* which the user will load at the start of each session.

       Testing showed up various problems The date on the invoice had been inserted using Insert, Date and Time but this meant that the invoice always shows today's date whereas I wanted it to show the date it was created. I solved this by using a CreateDate field instead.

Etc

Results of testing

As you go through the tests that you documented in the Design section, take screen shots or produce reports, invoices, letters etc which can be annotated by hand. The annotation is needed to show:

- What test was being performed;

- Whether the results were as expected;

- Any features that you want to draw to the attention of someone examining the test output.

For example:

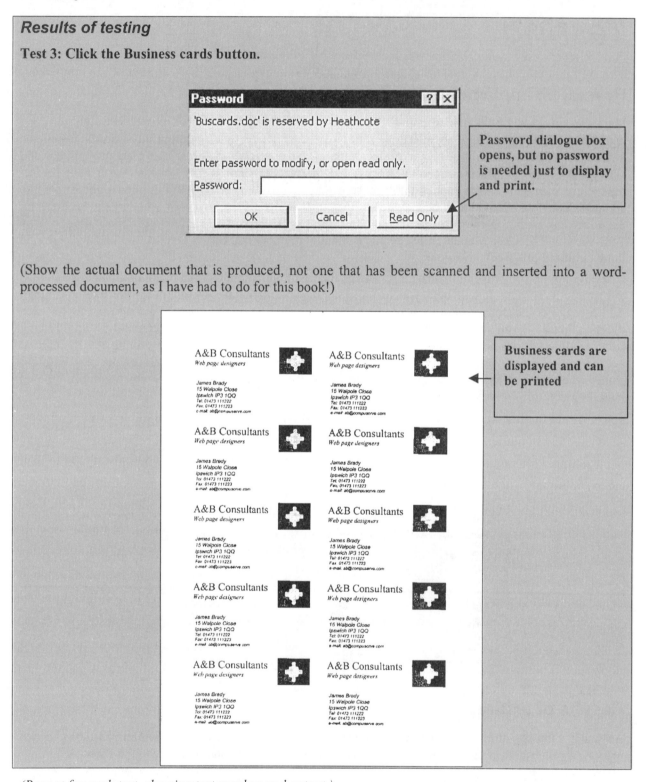

Results of testing

Test 3: Click the Business cards button.

Password dialogue box opens, but no password is needed just to display and print.

(Show the actual document that is produced, not one that has been scanned and inserted into a word-processed document, as I have had to do for this book!)

Business cards are displayed and can be printed

(Repeat for each test, showing test number and output.)

Technical manual

Use this section to enable a person competent in the advanced features of Word to make changes to your system if required. Do not use it to give a tutorial in how to use Word – you can assume the reader of this section is an expert. Explain where and how you have used advanced features. You can get a listing of each macro by selecting **Tools**, **Macro**, **Macros**, **Edit**. Then print out a listing to include in your documentation.

For example:

Macros

The following macros are stored in the master template ABNormal.

OpenNormal	Opens a new document based on the Normal template stored in the default directory. This is a recorded macro, used to get the code for opening a new document. The code was then amended to create OpenABLetter.
OpenABLetter	Created by editing OpenNormal. It opens a new document using the ABNormal template. It is run by selecting New Letter on the full screen menu.
Accountant	This is a recorded macro which first runs OpenABLetter and then puts in the name and address of the Accountant. It is run by selecting Letters, Accountant from the custom menu on the menu bar.
Partner	This is a recorded macro which first runs OpenABLetter and then puts in the name and address of James' Partner Jo Anderson. It is run by selecting Letters, Partner from the custom menu on the menu bar.
Supplier	This is a recorded macro which first runs OpenABLetter and then puts in the name and address of James' Internet services provider. It is run by selecting Letters, Supplier from the custom menu on the menu bar.

These macros are listed below:

```
Sub OpenNormal()
'
' OpenNormal Macro
' Opens a file based on Normal template
'
    Documents.Add Template:="C:\Program Files\MSoffice\Templates\Normal.dot", _
        NewTemplate:=False
    Selection.Font.Size = 24
    Selection.Font.Bold = wdToggle
    Selection.ParagraphFormat.Alignment = wdAlignParagraphCenter
    Selection.TypeText Text:="Special Offer!!"
    Selection.TypeParagraph
End Sub

Sub OpenABLetter()
'
' OpenABLetter Macro
' Opens a new file based on ABLetter.dot
'
    Documents.Add Template:="A:\ABLetter.dot", _
        NewTemplate:=False
End Sub

Sub Accountant()
'
```

```
' Accountant Macro
' Macro recorded 21/08/98 by Heathcote
'
   Application.Run MacroName:="OpenABLetter"
   Selection.TypeParagraph
   Selection.TypeParagraph
   Selection.TypeText Text:="Mr T.Dodger"
Etc
```

The following macros are stored in Maindoc.doc, which acts as a 'front end' for the system.

(List the macros, and explain what they are for. Other macros may be attached to buttons in various documents such as the UpdateFields macro in the Invoice template.)

User manual

This section is aimed entirely at a non-technical user and should use ordinary English rather than 'computer-speak'. For example, do not say 'Boot up the system' when 'Switch on the computer' will achieve the same result.

Presentation is all-important here. Use whatever facilities your word processor has to enhance the appearance of the document, spell-check it carefully and read it through to make sure it flows well and makes sense. It should be a 'stand-alone' document and could even be bound separately from the rest of the project. Your user manual should include:

- A table of contents;
- An introduction, stating what the system is about and who it is for;
- Installation instructions and guidance on minimum configuration needed;
- Examples of actual screen displays such as menus, data input screens and output screens;
- Samples of printed output;
- An explanation of what each option on a menu does;
- Any special instructions on how to input data – for example the format of a date field, or the range of accepted values in an amount field;
- An explanation of any manual procedures such as batching or recording data manually;
- Error messages that may be displayed and what to do in that event;
- Error recovery procedures – for example what to do if you realise you have made a wrong data entry, or the power goes off in the middle of an update;
- Backup procedures;
- Perhaps a hot-line help number.

If you have used a package, explain how to use the system you have created, rather than explaining how to use the software package in general terms. It is a good idea to test out your user manual on the user or a colleague to see if they can follow your instructions without any extra help from you.

For example:

Introduction

Welcome to the A&B Consultants customised Word system. It will enable you to carry out your day-to-day word-processing in the most efficient and time-saving way possible, using customised menus and toolbars to load templates specially created for your needs.

To access the customised system, load the document *Maindoc* from the default directory **My Documents**.

Main menu

When you have loaded *Maindoc*, click the **Display** menu button on the menu bar next to **Help**. This will cause the main menu to be displayed, and you will see the following screen.

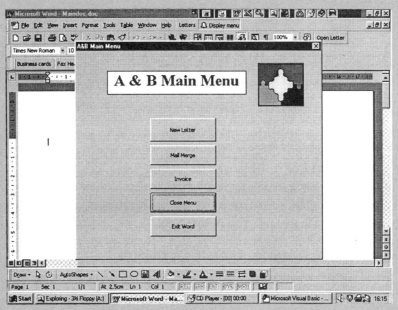

Figure 21.1: Main menu in User manual

The A&B toolbar

You will also see a custom toolbar called the A&B toolbar appear under the other toolbars, with buttons for **Business cards, Fax Header, With Comps** and **Headed stationery**.

These buttons are used to display stationery that you need to print out.

The Letters menu on the menu bar

The **Letters** menu has three options: **Accountant, Partner and Supplier**. When you want to write a letter to your accountant, for example, click on **Letters** and choose **Accountant**. A new letter will appear with Mr Dodger's name and address already inserted.

The main menu

The main menu has 5 options. It closes automatically when for example you load a new letter, but it can be redisplayed at any time by clicking the **Display menu** button on the menu bar. Each of the menu options will now be described.

(etc).

Other user help systems

As well as a user manual, you might think about providing the user with on-line help. By putting bookmarks in a document you can create a hyperlink to jump directly to a particular help topic stored in a separate Help file. Look up Task 11.2 for more information on how to do this.

Chapter 22 – Evaluation

Introduction

The final section of the project is the evaluation, accounting for some 20% of the total mark. This is where you compare what you set out to do with what you have achieved and write an honest appraisal of your efforts. It should be clearly related to the list of specific objectives written in the Analysis section. The more clearly you have stated the objectives, the easier it will be to evaluate how well your system achieved them.

Writing the evaluation

If the project has been written for a real user, it is a good idea to include the user's comments in this section, perhaps in the form of a letter written on official headed paper and signed by the user. If any suggestions have been made for amendment or improvement, include these as well, whether or not you have managed to incorporate the suggestions. Add your own suggestions for improvement and possibilities for future development. Do take note that a fake letter from your best friend or a glowing letter from an uncritical parent stating how marvellous your system is, flying in the face of all the evidence, is not likely to gain you any marks.

Be honest about the shortcomings of the project; if it is not complete, maybe this is because it was over-ambitious and you should say so. You will not, however, score many marks for criticising the hardware, software, staff or lack of time. One of the skills to be learned in writing a project is to finish it on time in spite of all the difficulties you may encounter!

Honesty pays – if the project has some apparent failures, turn these into successes and gain credit showing what was learnt, documenting what was being attempted, what the outcome was and what difficulties were experienced. Your teacher can authenticate hardware and software difficulties that were beyond your control.

For example:

> ### Evaluation of how well each objective was achieved
>
> *Objective 1: ...*
>
> *...*
>
> *Objective 6: To be able to identify which customers have been sent a reminder, and to be able to easily amend records of customers who have paid and therefore do not need further reminders.*
>
> The original idea was that when customers had been sent a reminder, the **LetterSent** field would be changed to **Y**. However this was not really adequate as James sends out several different letters to customers including one advertising a special offer, and it is not clear from the **LetterSent** field which customer had received which letter. To fix this I need to add more fields to the customer record, for example **Paid, First Reminder, Second Reminder**. The **LetterSent** field could then be used for letters sent out at a particular time and the others for recording which customers had paid.
>
> It will be quite easy for James to add new fields if they are needed, and this could be explained in the User Manual. Also, it would be a good idea to write a macro to automatically set the **LetterSent** field to **Y** on all records after a mail merge has been done to all customers, instead of having to manually update each record. Another macro could be written to set the **LetterSent** field back to **N** before a new mailing.

And finally...

The NEAB recommends that the project report should not exceed 9000 words, which is about 20 pages excluding screen shots. You will not find it hard to fill 20 pages – on the contrary, many students find they have difficulty sticking to this limit. So don't waffle, don't repeat yourself, and be sure to read through what you have written.

Buy a folder of some kind (NOT a ring binder which cannot easily be posted to the moderator) and hand in a really professional-looking report. It's important to bind all the sheets in the project together, by means of treasury tags or comb-binding, for example. Slide binders often make it difficult to read all the text, or they come off.

Appendix

NEAB Project Guidelines

Instructions and guidance on the internal assessment of the coursework Module IT03

7.1   Introduction

Project work is an important aspect of the Information Technology (Advanced) and (Advanced Supplementary) syllabuses and it will carry 40 per cent of the total marks for the examination. The projects will be internally assessed and externally moderated.

7.1.1   Core 3 (IT03) module

Two minor projects are to be completed. 20 per cent of the total marks for the examination will be allocated to the minor projects, 10 per cent to each.

7.1.2   Extension 3 (IT06) module

One major project is to be completed. 20 per cent of the total marks for the examination will be allocated to the major project.

7.2

It should be noted that the project reports will subsequently be scrutinised by a moderator who may have no knowledge of the packages used by the candidate or the background to the problem tackled.

Documentation and annotated evidence must therefore provide sufficient information for the moderator to be able to assess the work. The candidate's teacher will be expected to note on the *Candidate Internal Assessment Form* the nature of any assistance given and the extent to which any given solution actually works as stated in the reports.

7.3   The nature of the project work

The projects will assess the candidate's ability to use information technology tools and techniques to solve real and realistic problems.

7.3.1   In the two minor projects emphasis will be on the full exploitation of particular generic application software and the advanced facilities available within them.

7.3.2   The major project will normally be assessed at the end of the course and will serve as an opportunity for the candidate to draw upon and integrate the skills and concepts developed throughout the course.

7.4

The problems tackled in the projects should, ideally, emerge from the candidates' studies in other curriculum areas, or from their interests or actual experiences in other activities.

7.5   All projects should

7.5.1   involve the use by candidates of appropriate aspects of information technology throughout its various stages,

7.5.2   involve real problems which have been identified with the teacher or end-user. These may be in areas such as leisure, business, commerce, industry, education, home and community.

7.5.3   encourage small group/team work as happens so often in industry. However, if a task is to be part of the overall assessment, the work of an individual candidate must be clearly identifiable and capable of assessment in accordance with the criteria.

7.6   It is expected that candidates will, whenever necessary, seek advice and guidance about their project work. All such assistance must be acknowledged by the candidate and is to be taken into account by the teacher when making the assessment. The guidance of teachers will be particularly important in the early stages when candidates will be expected to select the most appropriate techniques for solving their problem. Teachers, when necessary, may suggest or may guide candidates to suitable generic application software. Candidates should be encouraged to keep a log book containing short notes of their work on the project and details of when guidance has been obtained.

7.7   **Choice of the Minor Projects (Core 3 (IT03) module)**

It is anticipated that teachers will introduce candidates to problem-solving techniques involving the use of a range of generic software facilities. These will include databases, spreadsheets, document processing and desk top publishing and graphics packages. However, teachers may well wish to introduce other types of software or packages and are encouraged to do so.

The candidate's teacher is required to assess the problem-solving ability of the candidate using two of these packages. Each of these assessments will involve the candidate in problem-solving activities largely relating to one particular type of generic application software.

7.8   In completing a minor project, the candidate will be required to undertake the following processes.

7.8.1   The definition of a problem in information technology terms.

7.8.2   The derivation or specification of information technology tasks.

7.8.3   The determination of a plan for implementation, which should be clearly documented.

7.8.4   The implementation and testing of a solution, which will involve the use of advanced functionalities of the package in the most efficient way to achieve the desired results.

7.8.5   Evaluation of the solution against the requirements of any potential user.

7.9   Candidates are required to provide a written commentary of these processes in document form.

7.10   **Choice of Major Project (Extension 3 (IT06) module)**

The major project will normally be assessed at the end of the course and will involve the candidate in identifying a problem requiring information technology tools and techniques for its possible solution and then selecting the appropriate tool or tools for the solution of the problem.

7.11   It is expected that candidates will carry out the following stages in the work.

7.11.1   Identify and research a real and realistic problem to determine the client's requirements and identify the role of information technology in meeting these requirements.

7.11.2   Produce an agreed requirement specification.

7.11.3   Analyse the problem and design an appropriate solution.

7.11.4   Implement, test and document the chosen solution.

7.11.5   Evaluate the chosen solution.

7.11.6   Compile an ongoing record, giving reasons for each decision made.

7.12   Candidates should be encouraged to make their own choice of project.

7.13   Proposals for projects, after initial approval by the teacher responsible for the supervision of work, *may be* submitted to the Board for *comment and guidance*. The facility is provided by the Board so as to reduce the possibility of candidates embarking on projects which are unlikely to provide access to the full range of marks available. [Centres are encouraged to make use of this facility, since it disciplines the candidate to focus on the required level of detail]

7.14   A list of questions for consideration by candidates during completion of the project is given in Appendix E.

7.15   Candidates are required to write a report on their project. This written report should not exceed 9000 words in length or occupy a word processor file exceeding 75K bytes, excluding diagrams and listings, although this should not be regarded as a rigid limitation.

7.16   **Supervision and authentication**

Centres entering candidates for Information Technology (Advanced Supplementary) and Information Technology (Advanced) must accept the obligation to provide sufficient supervision to enable them to give an assurance that every step has been taken to ensure that the work submitted is that of the candidate concerned. When a candidate has need of assistance in completing a particular piece of work, such assistance should be given but the teacher must take degree of assistance given into account when making the assessment and, when necessary, should add appropriate comments on the *Candidate Internal Assessment Form* (Appendix A).

It is expected that the teacher will be involved at the following stages.

7.16.1   Initial discussion at the time when the project is being chosen and work is being planned. The final choice should be that of the individual candidate, but the teacher will be expected to discuss the proposed choice of project so that guidance can be given about suitability and appropriateness before work begins. It is anticipated that such advice will ensure that the task attempted is neither trivial nor over-ambitious.

7.16.2   Periodic supervision and discussion as appropriate, e.g. discussion of the availability and use of material.

7.16.3   Guidance on the presentation of the project, including the information to be given on the *Coursework Cover Sheet.*

7.17   The NEAB recognises that the problem of authentication is increased by the nature of the project work. An essential feature of such work is the use by the candidate of the techniques of research and investigation, including use of abilities to discover information, to discriminate amongst a variety of sources of information, to marshal evidence and to present all the available relevant evidence as part of the presentation of the topic and as the basis for conclusions. The candidate will often be expected to search for, and utilise, information assembled by others. There is, however, an important distinction between plagiarism and the acquisition of information by research. The distinction lies in the use made by the candidate of the information obtained and the extent to which findings are presented as the result of his/her researches or as his/her own data or conclusions. To assist the teacher in the assessment and authentication, candidates must be instructed to provide a clear and comprehensive statement of the sources of information on the *Coursework Cover Sheet* provided by the Board. It is also expected that the teacher will make full use of discussions with the candidate regarding his/her work as an effective method of establishing its authenticity.

7.18   The teacher is responsible for warning the candidate of the NEAB regulations concerning malpractice. The regulation states that candidates are forbidden to indulge in any unfair practice in the preparation of coursework project work required for assessment as part of the examination. Any candidate who uses, or is suspected of using or attempting to use, any unfair means is to be reported immediately to the NEAB. If the Board is satisfied that a breach of the *Regulations* has occurred, the candidate will be liable to be disqualified in the whole of the current examination for the GCE, including all work completed before and after the breach of the *Regulations* occurred. The candidate will be required to certify on the *Coursework Cover Sheet* that he/she has read and understood the regulations relating to unfair practice.

7.19   Where the nature of the project work requires candidates to undertake some assessed coursework activities outside the classroom, some work must take place under direct supervision to allow the teacher concerned to authenticate each candidate's work with confidence. The work completed outside direct supervision must be identified.

7.20   The teacher responsible for the supervision of the candidates' work will be required to certify, by signing a *Coursework Certification Sheet* (Appendix D), that the marks submitted were awarded in accordance with the instructions in the syllabus and that he/she is entirely satisfied that the work submitted is that of the candidate concerned.

7.21   **Marking and Standardising of project work**

It is necessary to provide a structure for the assessment of project work so that all teachers are, in general, following a common procedure. Such a procedure will assist with the standardisation of assessment from centre to centre. Each project is therefore to be assessed in accordance with the guidelines set out below. In assessing candidates, centres must ensure that comparable standards are observed between different teaching groups. Each centre must produce a single order of merit for the centre as a whole.

Criteria for the assessment of the minor projects

7.22   The following categories are to be used in the assessment of each minor project. The criteria for marking these categories are listed below. Each minor project is marked out of a total of 45.

Analysis And Design (13 marks)

10-13   A detailed requirements' specification has been produced and used as the basis for the derivation of input, processing and output needs. The analysis and design show in detail what is required to carry out the task in a comprehensive manner - this can include layout sheets, record structures, spreadsheet plans, design for data-capture sheets, data modelling, etc as appropriate.

The design indicates an appreciation of the full potential of the appropriate hardware and software facilities and human resources available and also, if appropriate, their limitations. There is an explicit statement of how the named applications package is to be used. The design could be used by a competent person for implementation.

An effective and full testing plan has been devised including the test data and expected outcomes. This plan relates to the requirements' specification and includes appropriate evaluation criteria.

A well-defined schedule of activities has been included.

The analysis and design has been carried out without direct help.

5-9   An outline requirements' specification has been produced but lacks detail and clarity. Input and processing requirements are present but not clear.

The design states which applications package will be used but it may not be explicit about how the software will be used. Design layouts etc are present but show limited appreciation of the needs of the user and the scope of the software. The solution could be implemented with some additional planning and design.

A testing plan is present but is limited in scope or may not relate directly to the specification.

A schedule of activities is present but may be lacking in detail or may be unrealistic. There is only a limited indication of the appropriate facilities to be used.

The candidate may have required some direct help.

1-4   The requirement specification is vague, may be missing or is a restatement of the problem given. There are few, if any, indications of what must be done to carry out the task. Layout sheets etc are simplistic or missing. There is little indication of how the named software will be used.

The testing plan is vague or missing. The solution could not be implemented without major additional planning and design.

The activity schedule is superficial. The candidate required much direct help.

0   The candidate has produced no analysis or design.

Implementation And Testing (23 marks)

18-23   The candidate has fully implemented the design unaided and with no obvious defects. The system works and is an effective model.

        Many advanced facilities of the software and hardware available were used as appropriate.

        The candidate has shown insight in demonstrating effective test data to cover most or all eventualities. Testing is exhaustive and results of testing are fully documented. The candidate has provided detailed user and technical documentation.

12-17   The candidate has implemented the essential elements of the design reasonably effectively and largely unaided. The system works and is effective but has limitations in efficiency.

        The fundamental facilities of the software and hardware available were used in an appropriate manner.

        The candidate has demonstrated a range of appropriate test data. There is hard copy evidence of testing, cross-referenced to the testing plan. The candidate has provided appropriate detailed user and technical documentation but it is lacking in some necessary detail.

6-11   The candidate has partially implemented the design or has implemented the design but it is only effective in parts. The system is not fully effective and lacks efficiency in the design of the model. The candidate has required some assistance.

        Some of the facilities of the software and hardware available were used but not always in an appropriate manner.

        The candidate needed assistance in choosing adequate test data, and the system was only tested to a limited extent. The candidate has provided some detailed user and technical documentation but this was limited.

1-5   The candidate has implemented the design in a very limited way that does not meet the design specification. The system does not produce any effective results. The candidate has required considerable assistance.

        Few, if any, of the facilities of the software and hardware available have been used.

        There is no evidence of testing, or the system has only been tested in a limited way and only with considerable assistance. There is little or no evidence of a user guide and technical documentation.

0   The candidate has not implemented the system.

Evaluation (9 marks)

7-9   The outcomes have been fully evaluated in an intelligent and systematic manner against the evaluation criteria. Appropriate performance indicators have been identified. There is consideration of any limitations and the possibility for enhancement has been discussed.

4-6   The system has been evaluated against some of the evaluation criteria. Some, but not all, performance indicators have been identified. There is some indication of the limitations of the system and, possibly with prompting, a few ideas about enhancement.

1-3   The system has only been partially evaluated against the original specification. This may be because the original specification was poor. Few, if any, performance indicators have been identified. Discussion concerning the limitations or enhancements to the system are largely absent or have required considerable prompting.

0   There is no evidence of evaluation.

Index

Have you seen these other titles by P.M.Heathcote?
(Published by Letts Educational)

A Level Computing (3rd edition 1996)

ISBN 1-85805-170-3 Price £11.95

This best-selling book offers comprehensive coverage of A Level Computing topics.
"I have no hesitation in recommending this book to students and staff for its comprehensive coverage and its excellent style." – Dr Kevin Bond, Chief Examiner for A Level Computing

---

Tackling Computer Projects in Access with Visual Basic (2nd edition 1997)

ISBN 1-84085-001-9 Price £9.95

This book provides students with a comprehensive and practical guide on how to tackle a computing project for an A Level, AS Level or Advanced GNVQ course using Access and incorporating modules written in Visual Basic.

"Students following the advice and guidance provided in this book should be able to produce a project report that is worthy of good grades and also develop a real, usable software solution. Any project that satisfies these criteria brings the dual satisfaction of a good academic grade together with a job well done." – Helen Williams, Principal Moderator AEB

A Level Computing Study Guide

By Pat Heathcote and Kevin Bond
ISBN 1-85758-601-8 Price £10.95

Letts Study Guides offer year-round course backup, convenient reference and an approach to revision that really works.

Inspection copies of the above titles can be obtained from:
Letts Educational
Schools and Colleges
9-15 Aldine Street
London W12 8AW
Telephone 0181 740 2268